A WILDER VEIN

Edited by Linda Cracknell

Published by Two Ravens Press Ltd.
Green Willow Croft
Rhiroy, Lochbroom
Ullapool, Ross-shire
IV23 2SF, United Kingdom

www.tworavenspress.com

For copyright of contributors, see page 228.

ISBN: 978-1-906120-43-6

British Library Cataloguing in Publication Data: a CIP record for this book can be obtained from the British Library.

Designed and typeset in Sabon by Two Ravens Press.
Cover image big Alba photography/ Alamy.
Cover design by Two Ravens Press.

Printed in Poland on
Forest Stewardship Council-accredited paper.

The publisher gratefully acknowledges subsidy from the Scottish Arts Council towards the publication of this volume.

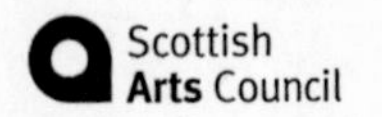

About the editor

Linda Cracknell has published two collections of short stories, *Life Drawing* (2000) and *The Searching Glance* (2008). She writes drama for BBC Radio Four and received a Creative Scotland Award in 2007 for a collection of nonfiction essays in response to journeys on foot. She teaches creative writing in workshops across Scotland and internationally. In 2002 to 2005 she was writer-in-residence at Brownsbank Cottage near Biggar, the final home of Hugh MacDiarmid. She lives in Highland Perthshire.

Contents

Foreword

'Culture is one of the two or three most complicated words in the English language', noted Raymond Williams in his brilliant para-dictionary, *Keywords*. He didn't mention what the others were, but I'd guess that "nature" would jostle with "culture" on the podium, along with "self" or "good". And not too far behind these, I suspect, would be "wild". A word whose meaning – since it slipped into Old English circa 725 as a synonym for the Latin *indomitus* (untamed or savage) – has bent, splintered, flipped and spasmed. Cognates for "wild" have included rude, morally insubordinate, sexually licentious, cruel, tumultuous, loud, impetuous, demented, foolish, fantastical, impure and uncontrolled. In the 1820s "wild" became the nickname of the Evangelical Party of Scotland: so a "wild man" was, extraordinarily enough, a churchgoer. Etymology, as always, illuminates – but here it illuminates extreme complexity: a torch-flash onto a tangle of wiring.

What are we to do with a word like this, then – this unruly word for unruliness? A word that's impossible to define, because its definition is a refusal to be defined. Best to embrace plurality, perhaps: let the word's currents surge. 'We should pray,' wrote the poet and falconer Helen Macdonald recently, 'for a little polytheism, as far as the wild goes. It's *wilds,* not wild. We need forty different words for forty different kinds of wildness.'

Just so. And over the past decade or so in Britain and Ireland, a body of written work has emerged that has tried to generate a polytheistic language for the wild: from wildness as state of land through to wildness as state of mind. Essayists, diarists, poets, travel writers, scientists and topographers have returned with fresh urgency to old, old questions. What constitutes good relations with a landscape and its nonhuman inhabitants? What is the effect of a sense of place upon morality and identity? How does place archive memory, and memory archive place? What is the worth of seeing an orca break the surface of the sea, or a parakeet flock light up a London plane tree with neon? This collective need on the part of writers to address such questions has, tellingly, been met by a need on the part of readers to have such questions addressed.

Some commentators have assumed that this is a relatively new kind of work. New journals have been founded to house this writing; new prizes established to celebrate it. In fact, writing that considers the shaping force of topography and nature upon society and culture is among the oldest elements of British and Irish literatures. It reaches back to early Celtic Christian poetry of the seventh and eighth centuries, composed by monks for whom precise observation of the natural world was continuous with devotion.

There are fresh aspects to the current resurgence, though. Three things in particular distinguish it, to my mind, and make it a genuinely contemporary movement. The first is the way this writing admits pollution, mess and muddle to its vision. Gone are the luminous purities of the pastoral form. In this contemporary literature, peregrines roost on cooling towers, and bubbling rills are foamy with surfactants. The angelic and the toxic braid here: in fact, the detail of that braiding is the subject of the writing.

Secondly, but not contradictorily, this work is animated by concern at environmental damage, and at the increasing distance between human activity and natural orders (if such orders survive). The philosopher Glenn Albrecht has written about the sadness that Australians are feeling as they see the landscapes in which they live adjusted by climate change. Familiar plants no longer thrive; birds and insects have gone, moved on by the shifting isobars. Soil, weather and air behave in unfamiliar ways. 'Nobody is being relocated; they haven't gone anywhere.

It's just that the familiar markers of their area, the physical and sensory signals that define *home,* are vanishing.' Albrecht calls this feeling "solastalgia" (from *solacium,* comfort, and *algos,* pain): a pining for a lost home. As a species we are now experiencing solastalgia as never before, and the new literature of place registers this experience, and weighs it. In this regard, unexpectedly, it can be thought of as familial with post-colonial literature – founded as it is on an awareness of displacement and dispossession.

Finally, while this writing is broadly animated by anxiety and loss, by anxiety *at* loss, it preserves a hopefulness of tone. Or at least, a sincerity of tone. By which I mean that it retains a belief in the possibility of consolation from place, from nature, from wildness. It annotates and values those instants when – Barry Lopez's phrase – the land 'snaps us clean like freshly laundered sheets.' And so, estimably, it strikes notes of sincerity in a prevailing atmosphere of cynicism.

A Wilder Vein is a significant contribution to this contemporary literature of place. The work gathered here is testy about piety, but not reticent about beauty. Repeatedly, these writers return to the idea that cognition is site-specific, or motion-sensitive: that we think differently in different landscapes. And therefore, more radically, that certain thoughts might be possible only in certain places, such that when we lose those places, we are losing kinds of imagination as well.

Robert Macfarlane
Cambridge, 2009

Introduction

As this anthology began its life in November 2008, I was startled out of sleep twice in one week by stories on Radio Four's *Today* programme. Amidst dream-muddled reports, the first alarm call sounded: a Wal-Mart store attendant had been trampled to death by a flood of bargain hunters unleashed into a Long Island store at 5 a.m.

'They're savages,' said a bystander. 'Savages.'

'Stop the world, I want to get off,' I thought.

Within a few days of this I was awakened by a report from Iceland. Jobs were being lost at a rate of up to 5,000 a month in a population of only 300,000, shaking the usually placid populace into minority civil unrest. But that wasn't the story. The economic crisis had coincided with a huge increase in 'ice-swimming', in which people run, screaming, into Reykjavik harbour at night. A spokesman at the harbour said: 'My theory is that we are so fed up with these people in suits that we want to be where people are not wearing suits. And where is better than in the ocean, where you take off your clothes?'

It struck me that these swimmers were perhaps the true 'savages' of that week, defined by being in a state of nature, plunging themselves into the here and now, and were a cause for greater hope. This anthology takes a similar plunge, away from consumerism towards immersion in the wild places of Britain and Ireland. The writings introduce us to some remarkable landscapes but collectively they speak at least as much of what it means to be human at this point in our history, and of how we seek reminders of our place in the world.

The landscapes explored congregate towards our northern latitudes and span west to east between the coasts of Donegal and Yorkshire. These are places of extreme weather, particular qualities of light; they include less populated lands of exile and ghosts. Stone, wood and water abound, as you would expect; sky, sea, river, mountain. We travel to shores and edges – marginal and liminal thresholds where the elements bite back, or our famously changeable weather brings a sudden sense of foreignness. The writers frequently profess ignorance in the face of nature's complexity, are thrilled or unsettled by a sense of changed perspective, or feel humbled by their experiences.

Underpinning their insights is a restrained acknowledgment of the pressure we have brought to bear on the environment. There are moments of sadness, and an awareness of change. The symbiotic relationship between the human world and 'the wild' is explored in several stories. Particularly where they tell of attempts to conserve or enhance the wild nature of a place whilst making a livelihood or a home from it, they reveal complex negotiations and dilemmas.

These islands do not boast untouched expanses given over to a natural order. 'Wildness' might be determined by a sense of scale or remoteness from roads, solitude, or a perception of surroundings that are natural or unchanging in comparison to human lifecycles. Or it might be the light on the sea. Or a dung beetle going about its business. The diversity of the anthology demonstrates how different this idea is for each of us.

History, memory, and the impact of the way that landscapes are seen animate the writings as visibly as the lines of river, stream and contour on the map. The pages are haunted by thousands of years of human activity which have formed our cultural landscapes, landscapes marked by tools or stones, by remnants of buildings. Some writers explore ironies – how romantic notions of 'wilderness' and 'scenery' can induce a myopia at odds with people's livelihoods on the land; or how the apparent emptiness which now creates a recreational paradise has sometimes resulted from great human cost and sadness in the past.

Personal memory surfaces as strongly in the stories as social history. There are loved places in this book, places which casket memories, that invoke mothers, fathers, sisters. Some have attached writers to a country or a life, some have launched them beyond.

The contributions here of poets, travel writers, natural historians, anthropologists and novelists give us many ways of looking, and varieties of writing. Amongst the pages there is lyricism and humour, biography and memoir, celebration and elegy. Perspectives come from inhabitants of these places, from visitors to them, from travellers from other natural and political contexts who find echoes of or distinctions from home.

The quality of intense looking by the writers, the curious eye, allows privileged insights which many readers who have enjoyed a sense of the wild themselves may recognise. And whilst not all of the narrators take off their clothes to plunge into icy water, they often seek the 'savage' experience, several exploring moments in which they are beyond the world of words, with time collapsed, enjoying rhythms which relate more to seasons than to years, to the cycles of moon and sun and tides. Engagement with places beyond the human-shaped often brings a different sense of self to those involved, provides refuge or restoration, or permits them to choose a way to live. The reading of these tributaries of sensation and being can bring refreshment to us all, coalescing into one slow, deep stream, that gives me the reverse of the feeling, 'stop the world, I want to get off,' induced by news of a trampled store attendant.

Striking images stud the prose: a beached whale with a mouth full of pebbles; a moon born like a gleaming egg out of a mountain top. But particularly entrancing for me are the lines which seem to accumulate through the pages: 'a curlew's thin thread of a call'; 'bands of white quartzite ... in broad stripes across the hills like landing signals for Martians'; 'a fine dense line' of pink-footed geese in flight 'dragging the speckled flock north across the valley'; 'great strings of music ... hung across the darkness'; swans wintering 'in straight lines along straight banks, like so many galleys at anchor'.

This abundant laying of lines feels appropriate both to a book in which writers throw lines between the invisible inner human self and the external bog and boulder, and to narratives of our long labyrinthine edges of sea and land. This book weaves a net from all of them, a net far greater than ourselves, and then casts it, to lay out its own map of mysteries.

Linda Cracknell
Aberfeldy, 2009

A Wilder Vein

Ardnamurchan Almanac

Gerry Loose

September 26th

It's just after the equinox. Tonight it's full moon – the harvest moon. This moon rises due east & sets due west. The length of a day is equal to the length of a night, but night, a cockstep at a time, is catching me unawares each twilight. There's a threshold here. From here I can stare into winter. It makes me edgy seeing the blackness in this morning's brilliant sun, reflected in the little pools of last night's rain left among rushes. Today's tides will be high & already the bay is preparing itself, with a calmness in the dazzle of sun, for the tons of water which will later pour in to cover its cold sands. The clouds are piled high to the south. Bare rock outcrops on the slopes glimmer, blink back in an unaccustomed brightness. Peat hags hold their water like the toothless crones they are, only tufts of bog cotton above on skinny stems. Pismires are slow today, stunned by the cold westerly. Ben Resipole's eastern flank hunkers in shadows. The last bee is at the last scabious flower.

October 5th

At the jetty & along, by the little wooden boathouse, there's no blue & white china fragments on the shore. The crackling blue shining of the mussel shells deceives, though. & the insides of dog whelks on the rocks, broken possibly by crows, are quietly luminescent, faint mauve & nicotine-yellow spiralling chambers. Fish jump clear of the water here, almost beneath the

Gerry Loose

Miocene otherworld gaze of the black cormorants on their rock, twenty-four in this colony, unmoving; watching wind against the tide. The small creel boats at moorings swing & fall & rise. The parchment grey-black leaves of aspens rattle onto the shore. Acorns drop & roll into the sea. It's how the brindled hound & I measure each day's incursion into another season.

October 8th

All morning Ben Resipole, Creag Dhubh, Bein Bhreac & the others can't rise from the clouds. There's no Sgurr visible to the west, no pointed Viking hills of Rum – Hallival, Askival, no Ainshval to be seen. The hound lies heraldic on the heather. Over by the parish church they slash & burn rhododendron understorey, but the smoke cannot clear the canopy, tangles in branches. Sheep amble past on their journey into the subconscious. While the mist hides, it also reveals: vast moorlands of webs, each with points of water at each intersection. There are two types of spiders' web here – one is floss & largely horizontal, but with diagonal digressions – sometimes seemingly random. This is all across the bog myrtle & up high into pale birches. The other kind is the geometric spiral from one branch to another of the oak & the rowan. The spiders must have (over millennia) adjusted web-building techniques to what they hoped to catch, if hope is not too farfetched a notion in the case of a spider. Like any fisherman, the mesh is larger or smaller according to the anticipated haul. Mist also amplifies the often unheard, the unlistened-to: the booming surge of the incoming tide & crescendo of curlews. From all directions, the stags' great groans of existence, their moaning lust for life driving them. Electricity volts through the hound's lead to my hand; she's seen them first – a stag & three hinds making unhurriedly for higher ground. Her ancestors sing in her blood, she trembles lightly. In another life I would have slipped her after them & followed her uphill.

October 9th

To walk across the coruscating mile of the bay in October sun, between land & clear sky, is to walk on rippling quicksilver. A heron stares at a limpid & disappearing rock pool. The pure, bubbling, unworded call of flighting curlews curves down to my ear. Halfway across I'm a tiny figure in reflected light, walking, walking, just one foot before the other.

a brindled hound
a lichened oak

Inside a wood, it is hard to see it for the trees which overwhelm with their forms, twisted, broken, growing one in the other. The curling holly finds shelter in the oak, rowans crawling decade on decade round the rocks send out more roots, grip tighter, a birch trunk springs back on itself in a slow double bend; a complete alphabet, a language of forms & lives. I find it hard also to see the trees for this reason. It's infinitely more complicated by the lichens & mosses. Mosses are knee-deep in places and year on year take themselves further up into the trees. Where the mosses are not in evidence, the lichens bubble across trunks. Ferns, too, in the crooks formed by the reaching out of limbs. & of course, the old nurse trees will have saplings growing in them. Sometimes it's possible to see what appears to be two or even three types of leaf on the one tree until the intertwining trunks, like ivies, can be separated from the moss & the ferns by the recalcitrant eye.

In places where we wander, say at Sailean nan Cuileag, the inlet of flies, there's no such problem for the hound. She's suddenly there ahead of me on the path, her eyes undeceived & undeceiving, she follows me, now to the east, then the west, ahead, behind, plaiting around me like a sapling alongside a veteran oak. She's perfectly disguised for this woodland, soft-footed, & in the October colours & light, all but invisible in her fur-lines of broken amber & darker brown. We don't take the same path – she has long delicate limbs, built for the speed of the chase, which would catch in the cracks of those mossy rockfaces I scramble up & down – but we end up in the same place – she's a gaze hound: from within her grace she can see my upright lumbering form as surely as I see the bunching leathery lungwort on the oak trees we pass.

October 11th

There's a solitary wood ant roaming the colony at the road bend. At the colony on the rock above this, yet more has slid to the rock below, but that landslide, that cityslide, seems abandoned. There's not a sign of the multitude of webs of a couple of mornings ago. We're all stunned by last night's heavy rain. The geometric webs are made by spiders of the Araneidae family. A study on Islay by the Biology Department of the then Paisley College, of Peatland Spider Communities, may reveal, of the 24 spiders listed, that some are orbweavers, like those here. I cannot tell. I scan their names but all that's revealed is the beauty of another language naming: *Pardosa pullata, Alepecosa pulverulenta, Centromerita concinna, Lepthyphantes zimmermanni* & *Lepthyphantes mengei;* the boldly named *Pirata piraticus,* the posing *Antista elegans* & *Silommetapus elegans,* & *Oedothorax gibbosus.* Some of these are the builders of the hammock webs I saw: moneyspiders to us. & for sure, they represent the riches of earth & the Earth. Orbweavers, money spiders, wolf spiders, together with other small fauna leading their stamped on & hidden lives, & with gastropods, literally bind the fabric of the Earth together. It's because of these small & slow creatures that I see each trunk a habitat, each stand of bracken or bog-myrtle a copse, a map of someone's territory.

October 16th

Andromeda galaxy, 300 billion stars' light taking 2 million years to reach us, cold. At 21.09 tonight, stags are belling through rut &, above the faint mountain's horizon, through the air-splitting roar of a low flying fighter jet leaving only its faster-than-sound anger. At 21.11 the jet returns, a little north. & passes round again at 21.15. There's a rustling in the dying bracken.

October 31st

Five days after full moon & still there's light through torn clouds greater than the starlight, looming Ben Resipole at the end of the road I'm walking. No lights but for these. All the steading lights are out across the bay; the stags are no longer moaning in Moidart or Laga. Late curlews waver their calls across the leaden sea at Eilean Dubh. The cold bites the bridge of my nose & I'm suddenly & unassailably happy & singing: the sign painted on the road bend is SLOW & oh I don't hurry; I step slowly into the night's mysteries & out across the turf under which a million infinitesimally small creatures lead their lives in the forever-dark, through which owls & bats swoop thick & noiselessly & the slugs slowly curve their way. Fresh rain drops on my hatless head; my neighbours the mountains dream on.

November 19th

I can feel the frost coming. The air is cold & still. Chimney smoke over by Kentra, not moved by any wind, drops to the bracken & rolls, spreading like liquid. The sky has cleared itself of sulky grey & the moon has already risen high. There are two sunsets this evening. One, the colour of an angry boil against a few delicate stratus clouds slips behind Torr Beithe, the tor of beeches, now conifers. The other, the colour of salmon flesh is hard against me in the sea by Eilean Dubh. A curlew's thin thread of a call as she rises stitches the two.

November 23rd

The hind moves on delicate black hooves over rock & heather, downhill, stopping to elegantly scratch her ear with her right rear leg; maybe, now in calf, she's in as contemplative a mood as myself. I move uphill in a sky rapidly silvering then greying as the sun rises above the bay, above Ben Resipole's hip & above rain clouds moving in from the Atlantic. The birches & the moss below are full of the flit & dart of chaffinches. The males echo the day, with their blue-grey crowns & rosy breasts, with the upcoming generation, or so I take it to be, slightly less coloured, but they'll grow into it. The female is altogether olive brown. A grey crow, one of a pair in an alder, is wiping his beak on a branch, with a knife-sharpening motion, to take off traces of breakfast.

Under alder & birch & oak alike, the skeletal remains of bracken keel & reveal the green vividness of sphagnums & the herringbone pattern & green corduroy of shield ferns, (*Polystichum aculeatum* is my stab in the darkness of my own uncertainty). In the oaks grow polypody – *Polypodium interjectum,* their green multiple tongues dripping & refreshingly free of cant.

Dusk comes a little earlier each night, bringing greater safety, but greater hunger to the deer. The Glen Tarbert stags are down from the tops; three of them that I see have almost identical broken left antlers. They're young & their rivalries are over, leaving only those cracked anti-trophies of male hormone flow, subsided as tide in the inlets. At Camas a' Choirce, a solitary fossicking badger trots & snuffles between pounding rain squalls, light on her feet, her belly low-slung & her body-mass index enough to frighten humans. Mostly nocturnal, she (I have no way of telling the sex of this animal) will spend more time sleeping in the longer colder nights, but have no food shortages just yet; the woods an autumn larder of roots, worms, carrion & mushrooms. At Kentra, young hind calves trot ahead of me, bemused by my torchlight in the pre-moon dark.

Clarity arrives with the full moon. Although there are clouds, the light is brilliant, lighting the white of sheep up on Gobsheallach hillside with a shining matched only by the luminescence of lichen rings on the rocks I finger as personal touchstones as I pass. Scale is confused in such clarity where I find it hard to ascribe anything but equal value to what is in front of my eyes wherever my glance falls – a lunar illumination scaled to fit human perception.

December 11th

A soft day. The southerlies seem to have brought milder weather, with harmless & haphazard smirrs of rain wetting nothing much. Matching that soft weather, I hear the calls of the ravens before I see them – a large silhouette flying across the hill just below my clear sightline attracts my attention & I'm momentarily puzzled when it swoops up as a buzzard. Then the two ravens appear & jink together, above & below the buzzard, sending it clear over the crest of Gobsheallach hill on an updraught of wind & curse. The raven pair then flies over to demonstrate possession of the entire south side of the hill. They might be performing a mating flight, such is their exuberance, wing-to-wing coasting, stopping short only of the upside-down flight I associate with their mating. But I guess it's too early for that & they are just whooping it up a little after their effortless eviction of the buzzard.

It's their gentle glottal calls I enjoy the most – the triple *hyonk pyonk donk* followed by a musical note like striking a dry emptied small log with a heavy stick, a deep xylophonic note, a marimba & mallet. I'm entranced at their flight & their bonded ecolect, their overheard personal conversation.

December 16th

With the very short days now, sunrise at about nine o' clock & sunset at about half past three, giving six & a half hours of daylight, there is more of the night & consequently of the moon. The waxing half moon rises at noon & rides high in the sky most of this cloudless day until it slips behind the horizon thirteen hours later at one in the morning. Plates of surface ice hem the lochans all day.

As well as the weather, of importance here is light & clarity. On this clear cold day, when every breath is felt deep into the lungs, there's much talk of how far can be seen & how clearly.

As the sun rises, the hills make one black & broken line to the south; in full sunlight, they resolve into three clean lines of hills, one behind the other, receding in distinctness. Even now, towards dusk it's still clear. To the west, the hills of Rum make a jet profile against a low band of coral flushing the horizon. Overhead the high sky is a translucent duck-egg blue. To the east & south the sun flares red on the hills, somewhere on the spectrum between the bracken & rusting plough at the grazing called Park & the flames of the fire burning the year's end scraps at the Kentra croft.

As the sun sets, the lines of hills become one again against an ice-blue sky. Clarity dissolves to dark.

December 28th

At night I sleep dreaming under goose down. Heavy in the

early morning on the peat bog I'm mazed by a solitary goose struggling to get airborne – a mastery of muscle & pneumatic bone over gravity – & when she's joined by a vibrant honking hooting cavalcade of score upon score, following in an untidy raggle of flight, up, yapping up, then for me, awake now, it's also willing them aloft to circle & make off celebrating life & flight; uplifting & uproarious all at once.

There's two sorts of goose here: the barnacle, all black & white, & the greylag, with its pink bill. This enormous gaggle is the largest I've seen; up to a hundred birds. I'm still smiling as the skeins make off to the south barking all the way; & at four to five pounds weight each bird I'm still lost at the power of feather-clad muscle; each of my watery steps across the bog makes sucking noises accentuating my weight, my pressure on the goose feeding grounds.

January 8th

It's not an escape here, but an engagement with the world as it is; something that's not entirely as we have determined it to be. It's just more apparent in Ardnamurchan that we have built over the rotting layers of sandstone & pitchstone, over the black basalt. Geology is obvious here, the topography where we settle in the hollows away from a climate predominantly of wind & rain. The woodlands have naturally been exploited and manipulated, the beasts & plants who live in, on, & around them exploited too.

This world, though, presents itself more clearly than elsewhere in a wholly built environment. It's as well to engage & re-engage with small sounds that punctuate the quiet, the greenfinch darting for crumbs outside the byre, the hirpling grey crow making a single note before rising idly away as I walk by, reed buntings *tseek-tseeking* their calls back & forth, sleet falling onto the bare branches & boles of the oaks. Domestic noises too: after the power-cut the click of the hotplate & the creak & groan of the heating kettle.

& the things whose noises I don't hear, simply take in with silent eyes – the white capping of each hill from here to Morvern, & north to Moidart, the glisten of the tidal flats in the bay, below which live the worms whose songs are of dark & of crackling salt.

I'm at the top of the chain that starts below the worms & their subterranean songs, a chain (rather a web) of mutual dependence, of symbiosis & clear ecological interdependence. That knowledge is a barn full of riches. It's also the wealth on which cities are built, & it's here that I fully engage with that.

January 12th

The Sgurr Biorach is the highest sgurr,
but Sgurr nan Gillean the best sgurr

Sorley MacLean

The rain & squalls stopped yesterday & the sky turned blue. Frost rose from the ground very hard, under a sky in which every star could be plucked & the Milky Way spilled itself north. This morning is clear & cold & the way to Aird Tobha is icy. The sun is about as high as it ever gets at this time of year & shining on the sea leads over to Eigg & beyond Eigg, to the little peaks of Rum. They are all wearing snow on their heads & haunches & from this distance, maybe twenty miles, are of a perfect & delicate volcanic symmetry. They are set in a clear sapphire ocean & lead me further, over the hatchery dams, across the tide-low sands of Sailean Dubh, over the inland machairs: inland only so far as they are sheltered by west-facing rocks. Where the tide has retreated, it has left goblet-thin sheets of ice across tussocks & over departed pools. Compelled forward by a need to see more of the islands, since I'm now at sea level, but with no sight beyond the nearest rocks, I move crabwise round Carn Mor, where the black terrier bitch that belongs here, to the man of the fishing boat, joins me. Like me, she picks her way delicately; frosted moss has a very thin crust. Where she senses a depth of water, she detours the long & drier way round. I move up & down, still skirting the Carn, past all the headlands – Rubha Fassadh nam Feocullan (which I take to mean the place of the pine marten), Rubha na Clioche Bàine, Rubha na Caillich round nearly to Rubha Mhic Artair. & there, when I finally get a clear view west are the islands: flat little Muck the southernmost, Eigg of course, with its own sgurr &, guarding it from the worst Atlantic gales, the hills of Rum. But to the north are the Cuillins & Skye laid out as on a summer's day, north & slewing round out of sight to the west behind the great sgurrs of Sorley Maclean's poem; Sgurr Biorach & Sgurr nan Gillean, Sgurr na Stri, Sgurr nan Eag & Sgurr Alastair with Sgurr a' Ghreadaidh; their names a litany of solitude & geology; places known best by those who live there – eagles, buzzards, ravens & crows – but which pierced MacLean's heart.

The way round the Carn is to move from the islands' stilling presence, eastwards & inland along the south channel, Eilean Shona to the north. I've hunted the small terrier away: I have no knowledge of how she is with sheep, & I'm heading for Fhaodhail Dhubh where the sheep wander at will. I cross the burn at Port na Lathaich with its little groves of snapped & dead birches, the sky punctured by the ravens' silhouettes & the rush of the water an arrhythmic counterpoint to the soft & melodious *prunk prunk* of the ravens discussing such a one as myself edging across the hill of the brush.

February 2nd

It's been snowing hard since yesterday morning. Snow has

settled all across the bay wherever there's no incoming tide channels. It's on all the windward sides of tree boles & in the clear parts of the woodland where I'm standing, west of the burn that flows into Sailean an Eorna. The trunks themselves are patchworked by mosses & snow drift, set against off-white lichens with here & there a snuff-coloured lichen on nearby rocks. Lungworts (Lobaria pulmonaria), also on the trunks, are a leathery green, vaguely lizard-like. This is mature oakwood, with a few fallen trees, sparse & interspersed with holly & hazel. There's a few birch trees here too. The fallen trees are almost certainly a result of storms, perhaps hurricanes. Some are split, the weight of large branches become insupportable in high wind, while others are toppled entire, with root-plates at right angles to the woodland floor, though it's seldom horizontal on this slope leading down to the loch.

One fallen limb, a metre round, is eighteen paces long from the main trunk, but still joined; it's a sessile oak, the main trunk a metre & a half round. Growth has been good from this limb, curving up & away from it, its recurving forms giving living space to a variety of epiphytes.

The oaks here have a massive beauty, fallen or standing, their relic lives entwined with each other & with all the other species of the woodland. Here, in a rootplate ten feet high (more than three metres) growing straight up, while the oak shoots from its recline, is a holly. It's more than double my handspan round, the displayed upper roots all elbows & knuckles, smooth as if polished. From the same plate is one of the ubiquitous birches, though smaller than the holly. Another oak, standing, has a massively thickened lower trunk, made that way by epicormic growth. Its girth is more than five metres round. Lying close by is another ancient of four metres' girth with a partner birch, older this time, maybe a metre & a half round. The bole of the fallen oak is host, under the snow, to a small holly, showing only its first pair of true leaves – last year's germination. Its roots will grow & assist the oak's subsidence back into the soil & rock from which it slowly rose. The ivies run round straight trunks, which subdivide fairly low into main branches. Each subsequent division curves & curves again, some so much that they seem to spiral on themselves, sometimes almost making knots.

I try to read the woodland, limb by limb & leaf after leaf. Its full story is conjecture. The epiphytes are an indication of ancient woodland, but it will have been worked here too, coppiced, perhaps, certainly bark stripping happened, & selective felling for charcoal. There may have also been plantings, though now there's no indication of this. The woodland, like all worked landscape, is art, & as such, fictive. If I'm expounding on the great book of the woodland, the lives of the trees, their history & economics, then each tree, in its subdividing & recurving limbs, is reciting genetics, performing climate & topography, geology & its own personal survival so far.

My ignorance is boundless. Not only can I not know the trees' stories, but the woodland itself reaches beyond history. I can't tell the names of the mosses & lichens. But I'm happy in my lack of knowledge; nothing at all can stop me from fully experiencing the setting & enjoying the secrecy of the trees; their utter stillness, which nevertheless they impart to me, here for a short while.

As I leave the oaks, just two feet from where I pass, & not at all bothered, a huffed-up goldcrest is bobbing & pushing her head into snowdrifts, below which are small plants' seedheads which she raids in her search for warmth.

February 4th

In the flat grey & foreshortening light, it's hard to see the hinds, unless they move. Although I know they are there, if they're still, & they usually are, then with the naked eye, even their white rear flashes can be mistaken for lichen on a rock. Their faded rust-coloured broken coats are entirely the complexion of the winter bracken, broken down as it is by wind, & curling that way & this after a season's rain.

The three hinds of this quarter, though, have been joined by another three. There's no stand-off, none of the stags' confrontational bellow. It's more irritation on the part of the original trio; they move on ahead, grazing, browsing, moving further up the hill with flicks of the heads & eyes & ears as the others make small transgressions into the precise margins of sociability.

The same bounds apply to all the gregarious animals here. The cormorants on the rock beyond Eilean Dubh are absolutely evenly spaced. If one lands on the rock, having fished awhile, the whole colony must needs shuffle sideways to allow her in, but without breaking the pattern of spacing. The chaffinches bustle about fallen seeds, but keep within the same imperative limits.

February 11th

After another clear-sky day, the moon has set & above me is an ocean-field of stars of all magnitudes. Even this third night of dark-walking, how little I trust my senses. Trying to abandon hesitancy & step out, since I know the paths, I stumble over every pebble, wonder at the nearness of rock & tree trunk. Soon, however, eyes accustom themselves to starlight & I'm aware of other things at the edges of perception: the squeaking in the ditch, which would suggest a small rodent unwisely voicing at my footfall; something that could be the slightest of draughts from a passing wing. I'm straining towards physical understanding of this blackly transformed landscape.

After the unaccustomed brilliance of the day where all has been psychotropically bright, especially the trunks of these silent white birches, walking with no light but the boundlessness of stars is moving from dream to dream. In all the runnels & burns is a sparkling from the light of centuries past sent by distant luminous gas to enliven water.

Night birds sing. I can only look up; I'm stopped & still, mind silenced by light. Light that's veering here & there into the red & green parts of the spectrum as those gaseous masses pulse like the throb of blood in my brain lighting my eyes.

There is no scale for this except, as ever, that of my own body. & its untrusted senses. I touch the mosses, I smell the drying soon-spring earth, I hear the whirr of a snipe as she plummets downhill. Tonight, mortality has a metallic taste at the back of the bared throat. But it's sight that's rubric for imagination, allowing through these pupils untold immensities of light. Of light which is a greed & a curiosity for every corner of life.

February 15th

> *The thing is, we get the point more quickly when we realize it is we looking rather than that we may not be seeing it.*
>
> John Cage: Lecture on Nothing

> *you who hurry toward leviathan woods,*
> *you who walk into the gloom of clouds and mountains,*
> *fasten up your raincoat, damn it.*
>
> Miyazawa Kenji: Traveler

Although I consider the soaring eagle to be a good omen for the day, I'm kept grounded myself by Miyazawa's words as I make off up the hill from the loch. Even after noon, as this is, there's pockets where that frost painting of bracken – a silvering outline of each brown dead frond – is evident, along with the woodland floor's resistant crunch as I walk.

It's axiomatic that if you go looking for the woodlands they're not there: just the trees. Once you've given up looking (& a lifetime is too short) then you arrive. Here, against the backdrop of the loch, with split rocks from which moss'd ferned birch & oak spring up like woody fountains; among litters of lichened twigs, broken from boughs by storms, it's easy to get caught up in the detail of the trees. Individuals: oaks with their leaders neatly snapped by gales, long fallen limbs debarked, each showing twists of growth round on itself; a triple-stemmed ancient sheltering a holly. Out of the burn's gorge rise hazels all keeled at ninety degrees to the slope, rising at right angles to that growth & bifurcating, a metre round, mossy, stretching for the light away from the always shade of the gorge. An ivy winds round a young oak, with its choking climb upward. There are triple-stemmed oaks, double-stemmed oaks, rarely a straight singleton stem.

Slowly, I realise, as I follow deer tracks through all this, brushing spiderwebs from my face, that there are open spaces in the canopy (even though the leaves are still only buds, the twigging above can be dense) & that in fact, I'm looking at a sort of parkland or savannah brought about by intermittent grazing. I'm seeing the woodland. I give a little shake, moving with the dance of gnats in the afternoon sun in one such opening; I notice the flitter of small fragile-as-dust buff-coloured moths. & there: even a red admiral butterfly fresh from hibernation, with its erratic zigzagging flight.

Among the oaks in this are hollies, which may or may not have started as infill among them. Sometimes hollies may predate oaks. Just on a small rise is a quartet of old fellows among the heather & fraughàn, bracken & ubiquitous moss, rising to ten feet up the oak boles; higher up are small ferns, perhaps the hard fern, *Blechnum spicant* (though my ignorance extends to ferns as well). These old hollies are almost within touch of each other; one's a five-stem with a stem dead, the next has three stems with two dead, the remaining two have healthy twin stems. They're like broken-toothed oldsters anywhere, sharing a rueful joke at the expense of youngsters around them. At their swollen bases is another indicator of spring coming from below: tender fresh leaves of wood sorrel, which is truly delicious & less vinegary now than at any other time throughout the year.

Birch & oak are indiscriminate in sheltering, here & there, juvenile sitka spruces, their seeds probably brought by wind or squirrel from the forestry plantation to the west. A small winged creature lands on my hand as I lean contemplating the mossy decomposing lines of trunks & rootplates. A dead oak takes at least a century to disappear completely, so these must have fallen at least fifty years ago, though the moss blanketing may have speeded up decomposition by a few years. There's a young oak, maybe fifty years old, liberated into the light by the fall of these prostrate forms, perhaps; but like any crone, bent backed, growing three feet up, then at right angles to that, then straight up again. In the hummocks & tussocks of sphagnums (how I've tried to identify them; always I come back to: it's a sphagnum, never further) there are birches sloughing their skins like any adder, along the lines of dead limbs all the way down to the floor. Moss seals & heals the lowest cracks; other birch branches from the same trunks are vibrant with new growth buds. The dead limbs, stripped of bark, demonstrate clearly the twists of slow spiralling plants following sun clockwise. Scabs of lichen everywhere. Growth in, around & on everything, sap-driven, moss-softened, rain-nourished. As many dead as living; as many wounded as healthy. A slow war of attrition with weather, browsing & life itself, even, especially, in February, bristling crawling & packed brimful on the woodland slope.

I walk & walk in pasture-woodland's own reverie, until the sky is streaked with cirrostratus over the egg-blue of morning & noon gone & the sun moves toward a Morvern evening to the west. There's the rumble of high-flying unseen jets; gossamer catches the low light finding its way under the heavy limbs. Oakwoods found & lost. I've been looking & seeing all along.

The Slob Lands

Neil Hegarty

The railway line runs through flat fields. On one side of the track, the fields are tilled here and there, rich black earth showing against the green. Green on the other side too, a green bank – but a steep one, topped off with concrete; and on the other side of the bank, I know that the sea growls and worries. But *I* do not worry: the sea walls were here before I was born, and they will be here too when I am gone.

So, at any rate, I thought as a child; today, needless to say, I am not so certain that these sea defences will stand the test of time.

I remember that we brought a makeshift picnic that day: a flask of tea, baps filled with ham and slathered with mustard; bananas and a brace of Crunchie bars. We had our walk atop the sea wall and breathed in the salty air; and then, in the warm lee of the wall, we had our picnic. Swans appeared, aggressively pushing forward for morsels, and were duly fed; a pair of donkeys were fed too, more covertly, with golden fragments of Crunchie.

These are the Slob Lands. An unprepossessing name for this expanse of Dutch landscape lifted and planted and pressed, like one of those rolls of turf that make an instant lawn for gardens, into a far corner of Northern Ireland. There are other slob lands, my father explained to me, because this is a name given to such places: to flat lands, reclaimed lands, lands that might be prairie or steppe but for the presence of water that seeps and flows and lies in the flat fields. There are drainage channels everywhere – the swans were lying in one of them that day, making themselves at home – and the water lies slicked onto the fields themselves. The same slob lands, my father told me, exist in Wexford and Norfolk and lots of other places too. I asked him why – why such a name? – but he didn't know the answer and I discovered it for myself years later, with the aid of a magnifying glass and the OED. In the meantime, the donkeys diverted me; and besides, it was enough to know that these were not just any old slob lands; instead, they were ours, and the capitalised sort.

Not that we live here, in the midst of this expanse of land; we are not farmers or rural dwellers: not any more. We just come here sometimes, though not very often. The Slob Lands spread out on the shores of Lough Foyle, a mere ten or so minutes' drive from our house in Derry; they lie off the main road to Coleraine and the north coast; and my father, who is often on the road, and who knows many of the nooks and crannies of this part of the world, will from time to time park his car at the end of one of the dead-ended roads in the Slob Lands (and there are many such, leading nowhere) and step out for a brief constitutional. He is one of the few: not many people in Derry appear to know about this landscape and still less bother to come here. These fields are out of sight and mind, crouched down on the other side of the hedges and to all intents and purposes invisible. Nothing much, surely, can happen in such a place.

And even though the train sails through the Slob Lands, they are too close to Derry to receive much attention from the carriages: the passengers are already on the bustle by this stage of the journey, gathering coats and bags and looking ahead to see the chimneys of Coolkeeragh power station, the first glimpse of the twin cathedral spires that mean arrival is imminent. They have run ahead of themselves, and the Slob Lands are ignored in the process. So you won't chance on this place; instead, you must actually come here and negotiate all those dead ends for yourself. I too would never have known of the existence of these flatlands, in spite of the fact that I was born and raised only a few miles away, but for the fact that my father had business in this strange part of the world.

I remember that we assembled our picnic, then, and headed for the Slob Lands, making our way down one of these strange, blank roads. There was nothing to be seen in such flat terrain: no views ahead and only tall hedges of hawthorn and blackthorn to either side. We parked the car at the end of the road, and scrambled up the grassy bank to the top of the sea wall and walked along, taking in the sudden, relieving panorama of water, field and sky. To the west, the blue Donegal hills and to the east, cloud shadows rolling across the green Sperrins. And I remember that the waters were not in fact fretting and growling against the base of the sea wall, for shingle has over the years accumulated and formed a makeshift beach: the tide was out that day, and so we scrambled down and crunched along; abandoned orange nets and bleached driftwood, oystercatchers on mud, and sharp gulls rising and falling on the wind. There is good walking to be had atop the sea wall itself: you can get in quite a hike, though perhaps not an easy one if you have a child or children with you, who might fall and split their heads open on the concrete, or slip into the sea. Good, though, if you have just one pious child, as my father did that day – or failing that, a well-mannered dog.

Two centuries or so ago, the Slob Lands did not exist. Instead, the waters of Lough Foyle ran in twice a day and inundated tens of thousands of acres of mud flats, and twice a day ran out and left the flats exposed to the sky and the wading birds; the maps of the time showed different lines, a different coast; Lough Foyle was twice the size it is today. In due course, Victorian surveyors came along and decided that the new railway line from Coleraine to Derry should run through a new landscape. The mud flats – all 20,000 acres of them – were reclaimed (imagine someone trying to do the same today) in true and impressive can-do style. Sea walls were built, the rivers and streams that ran down from the hills were channelled and bridged, their beds scoured and deepened; and in time, the farmers began to exploit the new rich soil that had been gifted to them. The railway was built; much later, the RAF established a new base on this inviting land, so smooth for planes taking off and landing; and today, we have the runways of a civilian airport too; a new dual carriageway. The Slob Lands made everything easier for the engineers, for the pilots, the drivers – and now for the dog walkers. This land is intensively used, in other words; we brought it into being, after all, and therefore we can employ it as we see fit.

When I was growing up, I used to set the time by the passing train. We lived on the other side of the river from the railway line and the sound of the decrepit train on its decrepit tracks carried clearly across the wide waters of the Foyle. The last service from Coleraine and Belfast pulled into Derry's Waterside Station just before 10 p.m.; if I heard it passing, slowing down just before the hour, I knew that it was high time to be asleep and would roll over accordingly. I was a regimented child, and this is a trait that has only partially diminished with time.

From time to time, we would take the train ourselves. Not very frequently, it is true, but Coleraine had Bishop's shoe shop, and sometimes a spirit of adventure would seize us and off we would go, congratulating ourselves on our intrepid natures – for it was an adventure for us, to use public transport – and an hour or so later, there we would be in Coleraine; say it quickly and it is done. Not that I had much interest in shoes when I was a child – but I did enjoy the short journey, one of the most scenic in Ireland. One half of it sees the line curve under the throat of Benevenagh Mountain, with its gold-glinting sheer cliffs and its gliders riding the thermals, and then run along the brink of the ocean itself, the white breakers and white sands of Downhill that stretch for miles. And more cliffs, and tunnels before the train reaches the reed-choked line of the river Bann, when the landscape calms and greens again.

But it was the first half of the trip that interested me, after my first introduction to the Slob Lands. The train sliced through those flat fields, past channels and ditches exposed to the vast sky and to the predations of greedy or perhaps hungry wading birds – not only swans sleeping in the fields, but Brent geese wintering, cormorants and oystercatchers plundering the shallow, muddy waters of the lough – and passed over the Roe, the Faughan and other streams whose names I did not then know, and all of them broadening as they reached the sea. The embankments marched like fortifications; and of course I had the newly acquired knowledge that these were true polder lands: take away these walls and the sea would rush in again, and that would be that. All we needed were fields of tulips, I think now, and we might have been on our way into Amsterdam.

What must have struck me then and what certainly strikes me now is this intense artificiality of the land. The very streams and ditches mark it out so, for they are Roman-straight. The swans winter in straight lines along straight banks, like so many galleys at anchor; and the hedges that divide the fields are straight too, for this is no Irish patchwork but a work of geometry spread large across the landscape. One might indeed be on the high steppe or prairie or the north European plain for a moment, but for the presence of water everywhere. There is the railway, running straight through the fields; and the runways for the airport and the old RAF base are straight too, and uncompromising; the airport's yellow 'Bird Control' van patrols ceaselessly.

They are lonely lands. A strange thing to say, maybe, when one remembers the trains rattling through on their way to Derry, the planes banking and landing at the airport nearby, the dog-walkers striding along the grassy tops of the sea walls and the farmers working their rich lands below – the endless industry. But true just the same: they are lonely. When I come here now, to walk for miles along the embankments and look out across the water, the loneliness and silence are tangible. It is the effect of the massive skies, I think, that loom above the flat fields and put all our small, fond human endeavours into perspective: beautiful skies, but overwhelming too.

These lands see many hauntings. So the local people say, telling their stories quite coolly: the lanes and narrow, dead-ended roads of the Slob Lands are no place to wander down alone after dark. They never would, they say, and they shrug; there are too many stories told. Some of the ghosts are dead RAF airmen: during the Second World War, their small, fragile airplanes took off night and day, making for the open Atlantic, their business to defend the convoys of Allied ships running for safety to Derry and Liverpool and Glasgow, and to spy out German U-boats lurking nearby, torpedoes at the ready. Too often, the planes crashed on take-off or landing, ditching into the fields or into the shallow waters of the lough; young lives ripped away long before they should have been.

And other ghosts too. What ghosts, I asked avidly one day, but was met with shrugs and brief words. Older ghosts, and more malign and least said, soonest mended. Do I believe these stories? Maybe not, on a calm, sunny day in summer, with the water still and the oystercatchers busy below me, and the vast sky serene and blue. I have noticed, though, that I tend to go walking in the Slob Lands in the morning; and that I have turned the nose of the car for home long before sunset. And these days, as the water rises silently and the shingle begins slowly to wash away, I find myself wondering what happens to ghosts when the terrain they inhabit is inundated, once more, by the sea.

Black Rabbits

Marco Daane

The night is moonless but clear. Slowly the darkness grows more intense and the gulls, so explicitly present at daytime, fall silent. Only a single lonely cry resounds, even emphasises the fresh stillness. Below, invisible, the Atlantic bashes against the rocks. The lighthouse beams become thicker and stronger.

Suddenly a demonic scream cuts through the darkness overhead: *'Kokko-huu! A-kokko-huu! A-kokko-huu!'* Flashlights with red and green filters throw their rays in the air, looking for the individual responsible, but it is already far behind us and silence fills the air again. Three minutes later a second one turns up, immediately followed by a third, a fourth and more. It's way past midnight when they start to enter in flocks, all of them producing these hideous sounds. The sky is filled with a large-scale, winged invasion of hoarse and heaving breaths, first creaking low, than again peeping high: *'A-huhhu-huu! A-huhhu-huu! A-huhhu-huu!'*

They arrive out of the blue and seem to rise from bottomless depths. There are accounts of people without foreknowledge who were struck with madness by this horrifying phenomenon. Labourers, for instance, who were sent here to work: during a single black night they became insane. They believed they had stumbled upon the spirits of demons.

Pembrokeshire demons definitely lay down the law during any boat ride in this out-of-the-way place. So much becomes mercilessly clear on the way to Skokholm. Pulling out from sheltered Martin's Haven the sea is calm, but once Wooltack Point has been rounded the currents and westerly wind take over. Skomer comes into view, the sky is filled with cormorants, razorbills and guillemots; and suddenly Jack Sound delivers white water. It literally runs through the strait. At seven knots the local currents are among the most treacherous in the world. The water whirls constantly here, wind may complicate things seriously and then there are rocks, reefs and maelstroms with names like Horse or Cable Rock, Black Stones, The Anvil, Crab Stones, Tusker and The Haze.

On the 7th of June 1927 the fishing boat that was to carry one Ronald Mathias Lockley to Skokholm was grabbed by the currents. It was in danger of being swept into the even wilder Broad Sound, between Skomer and Skokholm, but just in time the fishermen managed to steer by and manoeuvre towards Skokholm. The return journey two days later was terrifying: it took them three hours just to reach Tusker Rock in front of Wooltack Point, with the current 'roaring angrily'. For three hours they feared shipwreck on the rocks.

But those events didn't matter to Ronald Lockley. What did matter were the two days and nights on the island in between. They had changed his life for ever. He could think of only one thing: how to make Skokholm his home as soon as possible.

Ronald Lockley (1903-2000) strongly identified with nature and animals. Like many young boys he used to plunder birds' nests and collect eggs. This changed when a couple of fly-catchers built a nest practically under his window and raised two chicks. From then on he wanted to study wild birds instead of stealing from them. He was passionate about them, if not obsessed. A mallard flying overhead would be enough to remind him of his wish to be like them: 'You knew not how my fears you laid, / How you set a bound-up soul free,' he wrote in an idolizing poetic dialogue with the bird. It comes as no surprise that he was influenced by Henry Thoreau's thoughts of modesty and living amidst nature. Lockley longed for the same seclusion as Thoreau's in the woods, but wanted to be surrounded by sea. 'I wished intensely to become a Crusoe,' he wrote in *Dream Island Days*.

Skokholm looked set to fulfil this dream. 'I longed to be there with the birds over my head, and with my feet exploring the ruins of the buildings,' he wrote when looking across to it from the mainland. When he discovered that the island was for lease, he immediately grabbed his chance. In October 1927 he went to prepare it as the future home for himself and his fiancée Doris. Other than the lighthouse keepers, they were to be its sole occupants.

A gap in the southeast cliffs of the island is jauntily called South Haven: just a simple concrete jetty and a couple of large steps hewn from the sandstone rock. On the wall NATURE RESERVE is painted in both English and Welsh followed by a warning that unauthorised persons should not moor here. Beyond, a steep path climbs the island. Skokholm, measuring one and a quarter by three quarters of a mile at its most extended points, is a plateau rising up to 165 feet. On the top the path undulates between rows of ferns to Home Meadow, a vast plain leading to the farm buildings as if it's one huge, grassy farmyard.

These buildings are Lockley's heritage. He uncovered them, roofless, in 1927, and restored them single-handed. They're now run by two wardens and will be our residence for this week. Life inside takes us back to basics. The old farm cottage and an annex contain some thoroughly minimalist sleeping units: straightforward wooden beds with a mattress, a washbasin and a gas lamp. From outside containers you fetch rainwater in a jerry can for shaving and a quick wash. A bucket under the washbasin catches the dirty water. You just get rid of it between the ferns. Across the yard is one of the two chemical toilets; a torchlight is indispensable for trips there during the literally pitch-black nights, as there's no electricity on Skokholm either. Lighting in the living and sleeping units comes from gas lamps that produce a softly simmering sound. It's perfect for reading and writing. The cottage houses a communal living room. In a second annex, The Wheelhouse, are a large kitchen and dining room.

The block dates from the 1760s, when cattle were farmed on Skokholm and oats and barley were grown. This is fertile ground and the relatively mild climate offers many hours of sunshine. Skokholm beef was famous for its succulence and high quality.

On the negative side were the autumn storms and 'salty' winds – and the ever-present rabbits. They damaged the grass intended as the cattle fodder. Furthermore, while on the mainland infrastructure and facilities grew at a high speed in the industrial age, island goods and cattle could only be transferred with great difficulty and cost. Retail became ever more complicated. In 1912 Skokholm's last farmer left. The island was claimed by nature again.

Ronald Lockley was to revive its ancient agricultural economy. After repairing the buildings, he prepared the old garden for the future growing of vegetables. Lockley had no intention of living the life of a hermit. He had a trading plan in mind. Others suggested he should try traditional subsistence farming. This seemed natural in such a place: fertilizing with guano and seaweed, keeping hens, goats and some cattle. Indeed Lockley got this going, but to him it was a side issue. His plan was bio-industrial: breeding chinchillas. Ever since his youth Lockley had taken an interest in rabbits and bred them; and the little chinchilla was widely recognised for its beautiful fur. They would earn him a living. He thought he could make a fortune from them. No one could stop him.

But when the first chinchillas arrived in April 1928, he himself gravely doubted the feasibility of the project. The main problem was their distant relatives: Skokholm's wild rabbits. Lockley realised he had to wipe out the population to prevent them from mixing with his chinchillas. He placed traps in their burrows and hunted them with ferrets, as was done in the fourteenth century. It was useless. The Skokholm rabbits had been without natural enemies for a long time and had lost the instinct for fear. According to Lockley's assistant Dick they were 'lazy b....rs'. The ferrets got bored by them. Lockley slowly became desperate, but was fascinated by them too. When he tried to explain their behaviour, empathy was never far away: 'Why, indeed, should the island rabbits run about? Where could they run to, on an island? Each was as happy as it ever could be in its own circle of territory, where it could enjoy the essentials of life for a rabbit – enough food and shelter in the first place, and companionship and sex satisfaction as secondary desires.'

Skokholm visitors spread out over the island soon after breakfast. Most of them try to find a good place for the prime local sport: bird-watching. There are thousands of them here: cliff birds like guillemots, razorbills, fulmars and kittiwakes, huge cormorants, choughs, peregrine falcons and – favourite with all bird-watchers – puffins. Their prime realm is on the cliffs towering above Crab Bay, an area known as Puffin Castle. From the bird hide, or quietly lying down, you may come eye-to-eye with one, two or even four of these 'clowns of the sea' just two yards away.

In the north the island path winds like a trench through a sea of rolling, surging green land. In fact these bulges and humps are the exterior of a remarkable ecosystem. The rabbits have dug hundreds of square yards of holes and burrows here, but another animal has cultivated the landscape further. Every spring Skokholm's rabbit holes are squatted on a large scale – by birds. The Manx shearwater, a sea bird, is dependent on land from February to September, its breeding season. They nest and breed in burrows. Around midnight they fly inland – only in the darkest of nights when they're likely to escape hungry predator gulls. Then they literally go underground.

That's why everyone should stick to the trenchlike path here. Next to your feet breeding is going on.

As early as the second night of our week on Skokholm we experience the arrival of these troglodytes. There's no wind, and clouds make it pitch black. Just before midnight we hear the first eagerly awaited call: '*Kokko-huu! A-kokko-huu! A-kokko-huu!*' Walking towards the lighthouse we hear it coming from hundreds of throats. Clouds of shearwaters must be right over us. It's impossible to describe what their sound resembles, but definitely not that of a bird. Now and then we catch one in the beam of a torch and soon we find the first one on the ground. Seen from close range, these little birds seem most unlikely to produce such loud and monstrous yells. Underground their partners make a similar sound, but it's softer and lighter, a gossiping tone. Once united in their family nest, they both take up this tone.

One shearwater glides down routinely but fails to see us crossing its flight path. It bumps into my leg and comes to a standstill on the edge of the path. For a moment it looks around, surprised by this unusual obstacle. Once landed, shearwaters rest awhile on the ground anyway. They're easy to catch with a torch or a flashlight using a red filter.

Lying on my bed an hour later I'm alarmed by a sudden bang against an outside door. Among the ferns in front of the sleeping units sits a shearwater that's gone off-course. When

I return from the cottage with a red filtered torch the unlucky bird is still there, but on hearing others who come back from a nocturnal walk it flutters about ten yards further.

On Skokholm you cannot overlook these birds. During their two months of incubation they go foraging in turn. Returning from their excursions, they know exactly how to find their own burrow. It's then they produce their bizarre sound, as a means of communication and echolocation. Down below they grow just one chick. During the sixty-six-day nesting period they leave it on its own ever longer – until they don't return at all and it is forced to come outside, hungry, lonely and curious. After six days of flying attempts it stumbles to the cliff edge and makes its first flight to the surface of the sea. There it will be in its element and safe from unexpected gull attacks.

Having met the shearwaters, Ronald Lockley was confronted with a new and unexpected problem. For half of the year he would be unable to put traps in the rabbit burrows or send in ferrets. All he could do was build fences. It was a new obstacle to his economic plan, but it also nourished his old love of birds. When he caught Dick with trapped shearwaters he reproached himself for not having been attentive. From then on, trapping was bound by strict rules. Lockley's love of nature also drove him to forbid Dick to hunt birds of prey as he was used to do. He even protected the vulnerable young shearwaters from the rapacious herring and black-backed gulls. Lockley caught chicks that went to look for the cliff edge and carried them to their escape point in a box.

By 1928 he had published an article in the prestigious journal *British Birds*. He now began to observe the Manx shearwaters too. There was hardly any knowledge with regard to the bird in those days. Both he and the journal realised the unique opportunity presented by his position on his own island. Harry

Witherby, founder and publisher of *British Birds,* supplied the first bird rings. Ornithologists visited and lent a hand. In January 1930 and January 1931 Lockley would publish extensively on the Manx shearwater's breeding habits.

Lockley worked at the foot of The Knoll, a small hill that guards the cottage. His research method was quite revolutionary. He cut turfs away above several nests and created tapering edges in such a way that he could lift and return the turfs like a lid. This allowed him privileged insights into the intimate togetherness of shearwater couples. He even observed them mating. Sometimes he would remove the birds and their eggs temporarily. The intensity of this 'relationship' grew further when he started giving names to his research couples. They coincided with the characters that marked his research burrows: Ada and Adam, Bill and Bess, Carol and Caroline... Lockley's method became even more anthropomorphic. He liked to express the interaction between males and females in the form of a dialogue.

This subjectivist approach helped his research tremendously: it all became clearer, more alive to him, and it enhanced his commitment. Surely he could detach himself; after all, this research was about the species, not about individuals. Scientific journals would probably never have accepted his articles if his methods overstepped the mark or were unreliable. In fact, it was to the contrary. His research fully revealed the remarkable life of the Manx shearwater. Male and female are life partners, till death do them part, and return to the same burrow each year. Manx shearwater chicks have the longest nesting period of the entire bird world: seventy-two days. Lockley was also the first to witness the newly independent youngsters fumbling to the cliff edge and literally plunging into the sea.

Skokholm's Manx shearwaters physically embody the cycle of life and death. During spring and summer the adults provide a true sound spectacle when they come looking for their partners and nests. At the end of summer the island boasts a nocturnal gnome garden: everywhere young shearwaters are to be seen standing outside their burrows, on the lookout for their parents or flapping their wings. And everywhere on the island you see the birds in the form of corpses and skeletons: victims of ruthless attacks by gulls who relish the entrails and rip their prey inside out. There's a perfect souvenir of a Skokholm sojourn: a shearwater skull.

Shearwaters and rabbits continued to obstruct Lockley's farming practice. Then, in October 1929, the world economy crashed. No one then had even the slightest interest in chinchilla furs. Lockley shut down his stock-farm, the result of months of work and a small fortune spent. The chinchillas were replaced by nine sheep. They delivered wool and lambs for retail and occasionally meat for home consumption. Lockley now focused fully on a crofter-cum-shepherd existence. He looked after his goats and sheep and roamed the Skokholm plains on his pony Punch, the image of a Pembrokeshire cowboy.

He also accepted maintenance work at the lighthouse, using Punch for transferring cargo. To his amazement it earned him more in two weeks than six weeks of fishing could. The sale of articles also contributed to his income. Meanwhile he laboured on a novel and sent Harry Witherby the manuscript of *Dream Island*, a book on his Skokholm life. In the summer of 1930 Doris gave birth to a daughter, Ann. She was unable to do the same amount of work as before. Lockley was busy with all sorts of things and slept less. Life was a far cry from that of a Crusoe farmer.

Skokholm offers a perspective that most people seldom have:

the mainland seen from an island. The south coast of Wales stretches out in front of your eyes. It's just a mere two miles of sea away.

Closer at hand, it's birds, birds and birds on offer. Above Little Bay hundreds of guillemots and razorbills stand side by side, apparently glued to the cliffs. It's a true spectacle of nature: rows and rows of black and white birds on the ridges, their rattling sounds and the penetrating smell of guano mixed with the briny sea wind. Even more marvellous is the view at Mad Bay further west: a cacophony of crags and chasms, sheer red cliffs on which the ocean waves crash brutally, more guillemots and razorbills, and shags in the chasms. On the south side there's Crab Bay and Puffin Castle, with seals, puffins and boulders of rock. Lockley sometimes climbed the mysterious Spy Rock towering above them. In the morning, patches of fog glide along the crests, hiding and then again showing Razorbill Cove. When the rocky centre of the island below suddenly looms between the fog patches, they reveal an unearthly vista. One expects trolls or eagles to appear from hidden corners. Tolkien readers might be reminded of Middle Earth.

Inland, a gull colony guards the plain between the farm and North Pond. In the breeding season, this can be a battlefield of biological warfare. Researchers who enter the colony to count the numbers return covered with gull shit. Three or four gulls always circle overhead, screaming and apparently ready to dive-bomb. Harry the house gull is the biggest contradiction. Harry was found wounded on the yard one day and was nursed back to health by the wardens. He's been extremely fond of humans since then. He likes to sit on one of the two giant gate stones and hardly leaves the farm grounds. When I had just arrived and was in my sleeping quarter, Harry came gliding in to land on my window sill. Then he started watching through the window – watching me. Harry likes to observe people, coolly reversing

Skokholm's customary practice of bird-watching.

On Skokholm you live in the middle of a bird colony, amidst a few species you can't easily approach elsewhere. Many visitors come loaded with cameras, telephoto lenses, tripods, binoculars and telescopes. It's a real pleasure though that the approach to all things 'ornithological' is very relaxed. Everyone is free to do his own thing and nothing's organised. The only ornithological 'formality' happens after dinner each evening, when the wardens take out the bird log book and enter the experiences of the day. Nothing special, no fuss – just sights and sounds discussed in a fun way.

Skokholm makes you into a bird-watcher, be it just for the week, or hooking you for ever to the world of cliff birds, choughs and especially the shearwaters. The island's log books show plenty of ornithological self-mockery. During our week the running gag is whether there are cormorants or shags on the peninsula of The Neck. We're not the first to debate the matter: once an *Identification Day of Cormorants and Shags* was held.

The bird log continues a tradition dating from the thirties. Ronald Lockley's articles in *British Birds* gained significance and he intensified his contacts with ornithologists. In 1933 they advised him how to build a trap to catch migratory birds. Other researchers helped Lockley with the ringing and studying of the birds that were caught. One of his visitors was Julian Huxley, brother of the writer Aldous. Huxley was an experienced biologist and widely travelled, but Skokholm struck him afresh: 'Here I felt, perhaps even more than in Africa, the power and the independence of nature – nature that helps things make themselves, as Charles Kingsley wrote in *The Water Babies*.' He went on to shoot a film with Lockley on the gannets of Grassholm, ten miles west of Skokholm, that won them an Academy Award for the best one-reel film.

In July 1934, Skokholm was visited by the eighth International Ornithological Congress that took place in Oxford. Lockley showed the participants the birds and their nesting sites, marked with explanatory notes. Afterwards they praised the Congress highly, but one thing stood out: their trip to the seabird colonies had truly been 'a never-to-be-forgotten day'.

Meanwhile Lockley was confronted with his rabbit troubles time and again. In the summer of 1934 his herd of sheep consisted of 150 to 200 animals, but the rabbits outnumbered them probably fifty to one, and devoured the grass. Especially in winter they played havoc with it. He considered gassing the animals, but refused to do so because it would mean sealing the entrances to the burrows and thereby locking out the shearwaters.

In September 1934, Lockley reluctantly decided to stop sheep farming. '[...] I had, I believed, the true peasant's gift or power of accepting a hard future, of finding reward not in terms of money but in the joy of monotonous labour with animals and implements [...],' he later wrote perceptively in *The Golden Year* (1948). Alas for him, any form of farming on Skokholm was 'an idle fancy, a half-wishing, a half-expecting'. There were far too many problems, and he lacked money for serious investments. The sheep were taken to the mainland. In 1936 Lockley reintroduced them, but only by way of a small herd of Soays, descendants of a Neolithic race from remote St. Kilda. These tough animals, a gift of the Duke of Bedford, were adapted to extreme conditions and unbothered by winter storms or rabbits. They enhanced the wild face of Skokholm.

Lockley concentrated on his bird research. He travelled extensively to the Isle of May, German Heligoland, the Blaskets, Fair Isle and the Faroe Islands. From there he discovered the Manx shearwater's phenomenal radius of action. They appeared to have an infallible instinct for their home and crossed thousands of miles to return there at speeds of up to thirty miles an hour. In their breeding season they foraged in the southern part of the Bay of Biscay, and afterwards flew to overwinter on the South American coast. Lockley would collect his discoveries in his ornithological magnum opus *Shearwaters* (1942), the result of more than ten years of work.

Winter was spent in a house on the mainland, since Ann had to go to school. They returned to Skokholm in spring and left again in autumn. Skokholm became a nature reserve and bird observatory – the UK's first, supported by the RSPB. More and more researchers visited, although only ten or twelve were permitted at one time. Compared to these pioneering fanatics, today's experienced bird-watchers are absolute innocents. 'I remember one occasion,' Lockley once recalled, 'when our party had patriotically risen from slothful postures in armchairs, to stand in rigid silence during the playing of the National Anthem, after a solemn address by the Prime Minister over the radio. Half way through a voice yelled "there's an ortolan in the garden". In three seconds flat, the room was empty, the more agile members having flown through the window, and a moment or two later the bunting was safe in the catching box.'

❧ ❧ ❧

One strip of land outside the smallholding on Skokholm bears traces of human intervention. It's a slightly undulating patch of ground behind The Knoll, between the main path and the rocks north of Spy Rock. Its surface is quite smooth by Skokholm standards. This caught Ronald Lockley's eyes in the autumn of 1939. He was looking for a patch of ground that would be appropriate – as arable land...

Even remote Skokholm wasn't a safe place when war broke out. The British government anticipated a decline in food provision and started subsidizing agricultural activities on a large scale. The news must have electrified Ronald Lockley. Growing corn, keeping cattle on Skokholm: all of a sudden new opportunities were arising. This coincided with a successful experiment to gas rabbits with cyanide the previous winter. Only several hundreds of them had survived. A vast blanket of fresh high grass was at the disposition of an eventual new herd of sheep.

Lockley realised it was now or never. First, he closed down the bird observatory. He developed a ploughing plan for the island. He would plough the northern part of the island in any case, later perhaps more. A tractor was to be bought and he began the scything. He also built new fences for animals. It was still only September 1939 when a new herd of sheep arrived, together with two calves, some geese, chicken and pigs.

Lockley's plan was remarkable. Eight years before, he himself had concluded that such an operation would threaten the island's wide-openness, its wild flowers and heather. It would endanger the shearwater and puffin habitats, if not destroy them. But in his book *Inland Farm* (1943) Lockley wrote that he had started executing it without further reservations. His explanation was meant to be scrupulous but sounded only questionable: 'I wanted to do two things: to fight a hard fight on the land to make it a worthwhile war duty; and to observe and study the changes in the bird and wild flower life which the plough would bring.'

Now he could grasp his old and never forgotten dream of hearing 'neighings, lowings, bleatings, carts rumbling, scythes sharpening, maids singing at butter-making, labourers clattering over the stone walks to their noon dinner' on Skokholm again. On the field behind The Knoll Lockley planted potatoes. The following year they thrived.

Skokholm lies at the entrance to Milford Haven, one of the

world's deepest natural harbours. Further down this wide estuary are the towns of Milford Haven and Pembroke. They're invisible from the island as St. Ann's Head blocks the view. Beyond, on the Dale peninsula, things are different. This is a wooded coastal area with low cliffs, pristine inlets and winding country roads. It's an idyll – well, almost. Turn around, and you watch the biggest super-tankers sail in from the Atlantic. From behind them two giant oil refineries assault your eyes. They process twenty percent of Britain's raw oil. Their seaside gables can be seen from almost anywhere in these parts.

Milford Haven's potential as a harbour was already noted in 1940. Atlantic and North Sea war convoys gathered here. Pembroke Dock was home to the world's largest flying boat base. Later, some units of the invasion fleet awaited D-Day here.

This all meant that the area was vulnerable to German air attacks (which in fact took place). The War Office looked around for a place that could house a defence fortification. Soon a dot on the map between the ocean and Milford Haven caught its eye. Strategically, Skokholm was indeed ideally situated.

In June 1940, Ronald Lockley received an official order to abandon the island.

So there was to be no farm. Amidst mixed feelings, the Lockleys began transferring their animals and possessions to a farm on the mainland. There was hardly time for sentimental thoughts as they left their island paradise. On the 24th of September they had cleared Skokholm. Only the Soays remained behind, as well as the pony Sugarback who was to serve the lighthouse keepers.

No farm – but in the end there was to be no fortification either. It was never built. Skokholm bears no traces of the war at all – or does it?

Perhaps the removal of Lockley forced by the war has itself

left its mark. How would Skokholm look now, if his plan to exploit it intensively had been realised? It would probably be covered with fields and pastures, producing grain, potatoes and milk to be shipped to Milford Haven from a modern landing pier.

When you sit outside the cottage nowadays and look in that direction, this all sounds inconceivable. That's because we're biased. It sounds inconceivable because of the reputation of Skokholm and Lockley. The island is now a unique undisturbed bird reserve. Day-trippers are not permitted, as they are to neighbouring Skomer. And Lockley was a foremost conservationist and nature writer, a predecessor of Sir David Attenborough, and 'the man who taught the British bird-watching'. He was founder of the first British bird observatory, co-founder and board member of nature reserves and conservationist bodies. Anything else just does not fit.

But it's not that simple. History demonstrated that this island was fertile and had economic potential. The production of quality popular food there was not new. Technology to improve its accessibility would be ever nearer at hand. All it required was an inspired man to rise to the occasion.

And this man was available. In spite of his love for it, Ronald Lockley wasn't gentle with nature. Sometimes his dubious approach served his research, like with the 'lids' he placed on shearwater burrows. But partial interventions were just as numerous and even more significant. A little owl that he thought was too fond of storm petrels and in whose nest he once found a hundred of them decapitated, was captured, ringed and immediately (these are his own words) 'deported' to Bath. His sole argument for this was that he wanted to act 'in favour of the airy petrel'. Later he also strictly controlled the size of the gull colony, predators to the shearwaters. His explanation was always that these birds were not native to Skokholm – a most unconvincing and of course totally subjective notion, which Lockley himself executed inconsistently. When the chinchillas had become redundant he released a number of them who mingled with the wild rabbits. There are still rabbits running around on Skokholm with almost black fur.

Nature once hit back when he assaulted it thoughtlessly. In 1939 Buckingham Palace requested him to arrange a 'pet auk' for the princesses Elizabeth and Margaret. Lockley was honoured, executed the task rapidly and made his way to the Palace. The handing over of the bird was the subject of one of Britain's first live television coverages. Therefore the happy few who possessed a set watched Lockley opening the basket and being 'ignominiously bitten' by the auk.

This may seem a funny anecdote, but it's an uneasy metaphor too. Lockley and nature did bite at each others' tails. He was aware that he didn't deal very consistently and justly with the landscape and environment of 'his' island. The traces of the chinchilla debacle in his books demonstrate this.

In *Dream Island* (1930) he distanced himself from the chinchilla project: 'In the future my income must come from the products of the island: from rabbits, fish and the future farm. To produce most of my foodstuffs was the ideal to aim at, and to achieve as much independence as possible.' Then, in 1938, in an article for *National Geographic Magazine,* he mixed the chinchilla experiment with the notion of self-sustainability. The farm, he explained, had been a part of that approach. In *The Way to an Island* (1941) he specified that: '[...] we had also decided to try to make enough money to assure the future and buy the island in the time allowed us by our lease.'

But in *Shearwaters* (1942) he erased all these views. What's more, the whole agricultural episode was removed. This was his most important book to date and he apparently wanted to leave an image of a Crusoe who was one with nature: 'I wished to settle on this remote Welsh island in order to live simply and undisturbed and alone, but in the company of those things I most cared for: wild birds and animals, wild flowers, the sea, and a wide horizon. [...] However, I myself did not propose to set up anything so cumbrous and unremitting as a farm on the island. [...] All I cared was to fit into the environment, to build, like the birds, a weather-proof shelter or nest sufficient for my immediate needs; and to obtain, like the birds, a plain living from the island and the sea around it.'

He must have realised that he would not be able to maintain this self-denial and modification of history in the long run, because in *Inland Farm* (1943) he was the Skokholm farmer again. But not until two decades after the war, when his island life had disappeared in the mists of time, would he admit the truth. In 1964 his famous *The Private Life of the Rabbit* appeared. In it he recalled how he had hoped to earn a fortune with the chinchillas. He had no choice then: the chinchilla project had more or less led to the rabbit research that culminated in this very book.

In the course of years these developments have all but disappeared from Ronald Lockley's biography. His intervention in nature and reconstruction of the environment do not fit with the image of birding pioneer and conservationist. He opened his eyes to that himself. He came to realise how risky his treatment of the island had been – although the question remains whether he would have done so without the intervention of the war.

In those years of neglect, Skokholm had returned to its former state. There were as many rabbits as before: the population 'had been saved by a madman' (Hitler) and had enjoyed a free rein. When Lockley returned, he was struck by the same remarkable cohabitation of rabbits, seabirds and plants he had encountered in 1927: the rabbits cut short the grass and kept it accessible, ignored the wild flowers (unlike the sheep) and dug burrows for puffins and shearwaters to breed in. This sudden confrontation with the wild Skokholm of old after a long absence must surely have made him realise how paradoxical his plans had been. His happiness at living on Skokholm was derived from the absence of civilisation, and he had tried to introduce just that.

Skokholm's complicated ecosystem was too small for two worlds, especially for the one he had had in mind. He could easily try to create that elsewhere. As for himself, he realised, one post-war day when returning from a scientific expedition, that he 'was essentially a peasant'. He was to remain one, combining farm work with continued research and writing. Painful as it may have been, he was able to reason with himself to accept the end of his Crusoe existence.

His fight with both nature and his own aspirations had come to an end. So had Skokholm's balancing act on the scale between the wild and the cultivated.

In 1946 Lockley handed over the Skokholm lease to what is now the Wildlife Trust. With various forms of support the bird observatory was restarted. The seventy-five or so remaining Soays were culled or moved off the island after a drought at the end of the fifties. The last of the Mohicans were the descendants of the goats kept by both Lockley and lighthouse keepers. 'They looked well in the rugged landscape,' former warden Jean Lawman wrote, 'and were to me a symbol of a wild type of freedom seldom attained by previously domesticated animals.' In 1981, though, they had to be moved because of their bad physical condition. When the lighthouse was automated two years on, no permanent inhabitant was left. Since then Lockley's Skokholm rhythm remains the island practice: it's inhabited from March to October by two regular wardens and weekly changing visitor groups.

Lockley remained actively involved with Skokholm as ornithologist and researcher. He also came to see the rabbits, no longer his enemies, with different eyes. On Skokholm he had already gathered a huge amount of information on the animals when observing them in a glass-walled burrow he had built. On the Orielton estate he continued this research intensively. It culminated in his epoch-making *The Private Life of the Rabbit* (1964), later also inspiring Richard Adams' bestseller *Watership Down.*

These and other books earned him lasting fame for popularising nature. Lockley also edited *Nature in Wales* and contributed to the Pembrokeshire Coast National Park and its trail, since used by thousands of walkers. He continued to live on the Welsh coast and various other British locations. Finally, he distanced himself from politics when the oil refineries were built that disfigured Pembrokeshire's bucolic landscape. In 1970 he moved as far away as he possibly could: to New Zealand.

The year before this he had written *The Island,* the most subdued of all his books on Skokholm. The island itself was its protagonist, not him. He narrated the history of his life upon it objectively.

On the right of the front door the outside wall of the cottage carries a plaque for RONALD MATHIAS LOCKLEY/8 NOVEMBER 1903-12 APRIL 2000/NATURALIST, AUTHOR, SCIENTIST AND FARMER, followed by words of appreciation and the opening lines of *Dream Island.* This small memorial was placed here on the 1st of June 2001, following a special ceremony.

The buildings had been painted freshly for the occasion. A group of Lockley's friends and relatives was welcomed, notably his grandson Bill from Canada, relatives from New Zealand and the US, the daughter of Skokholm's first cook, representatives of Orielton – and Ann, Lockley's daughter who had grown up on Skokholm.

'R.M. Lockley's final journey, back home to Skokholm,' the guestbook reports on this day. More than a year after he died in Auckland on the 12th of April 2000 his ashes were brought to the island. It had been Lockley's last wish that they were to be scattered on Skokholm. This was executed on the most fitting location: The Knoll, where Lockley had observed Adam, Ada and his other first shearwaters.

So how deep can love for a place root in one's soul? In 1988 Lockley had been present on the island for the Prince of Wales' visit. He wrote after his name in the guestbook: *'coming home again'*. Even stronger evidence of this enduring relation was his *absence*. In July 1973 Lockley accompanied a television crew that shot a documentary movie about him. The then-warden Jean Lawman wrote that he was 'as elusive as he could possibly be': '[…] the most common phrase heard that week was an impatient "where's Ronald".' He appeared to be unmoved and reserved, but this probably covered up his solitary, personal reliving of the island. On the 27th of July Jean Lawman quoted someone's exclamation in the log books that sums it all up: *'Mr Lockley had a shearwater in the toilet.'*

⁂

Nowadays the old potato field beyond The Knoll is overgrown by ferns again; only the smoothness of the surface is evidence of a human hand that once wanted more. Skokholm has been returned to the rabbits and the birds. In 1976 the practice of bird ringing was discontinued; the owner called it a day. Since then Skokholm is no longer a formal bird observatory, although research still takes place.

Now it's in need of nothing or no one to secure its identity. Skokholm is a child to nature. Its mother rules: the tides, currents and wind dictate the rhythm. These rules are still capable of cutting off the island from the outside world – but it might be better to state that it is *always* cut off from the outside world. Skokholm appears to have buildings and bird hides, but in reality they are islands on an island. The island *is* nature and visitors may share it for a week with the birds and rabbits. They come as close to mingling with them as is possible, but not more than that. They must stay in their own man-made islands and they must leave irrevocably, although the logs contain several stories of visitors who were forced to stay longer – by Mother Nature herself.

From the island you can see the mainland, you're aware of the physical distance. But psychologically, the mainland can be many miles away. Skokholm is a microcosm: it was developed in isolation and still everyone, visitor or warden, is contained here. And there's nothing to do but walking, bird-watching and reading or writing – like Ronald Lockley in his best days. Everything depends on nature's pulse and temper. When it rains or a storm blows, you just have the cottage and your company – there is *no* escape.

This is precisely why it fully absorbs you. First a kind of woolly calmness takes hold of you. The restrictions and simplicities of life, the complete absence of pretensions force you to a complete standstill. You do nothing at all – and at the same time you do a lot. For your mind still works, and after a while it even runs at full speed – but differently, much more intensely than in the artificial whirlpool called 'western culture'. Consciousness and comprehension now focus on the only thing at hand. You concentrate on the small piece of land on which you live, which for a short time looks like it's the entire world.

Next comes the wondrous feeling that this is *your* island. Of course there are others here, but you hardly see them. So you start wandering around like a gentleman-farmer who's looking over his estate – or even as a king inspecting his own kingdom. Lockley, who lived here for years, must have experienced something similar, even more strongly. As a result he nearly went too far in ruling over it.

A true king of Skokholm inspects his realm, and certainly his sea. In this bright space the image of the mainland can become a burden. When this happens the king turns around and walks to the other end of his world. Especially at night, when the king can't sleep, that is where he goes for the ultimate redemption. Even the few faint lights of Pembrokeshire are too much. He flees to the ultimate south-westerly point. On his way he sees the fingers of light from all the nearby lighthouses; continuous steady movements that are soothing compared with the frozen points of light on the mainland. And at the end of his promenade he reaches his own lighthouse, and beyond it the cathartic sea.

There, he knows, he comes close to the essence of this place. It's in the sounds. All mainland sounds are absent, and only the Skokholm sounds are to be heard. No engines or mobile phones, but the ocean, the wind, the birds, and now and then the Wheelhouse bell announcing a meal time. While the king's eyes linger on the black horizon, where now and then a pin's head can be seen glowing, he takes in all the island's sounds. The Atlantic wind whispers in his hair. In the darkness below, the immovable ocean strikes the cliffs with low intimate drones. And finally there is the sound overhead of the king's only companion. It echoes the perpetuity of this filled emptiness and leaves behind a notion of real symbolism – carrying the desire to return here one day:

'Kokko-huu! A-kokko-huu! A-kokko-huu!'

Quoted sources

Julian Huxley, *Memories*. London, George Allen & Unwin, 1970.

Jean Lawman, *Skokholm. An Island Remembered*. Tiverton, Halsgrove, 2000.

R.M. Lockley, 'Bird Observatories and Field Study Centres.' In: *The Emu. Journal of the Royal Australasian Ornithologists Union* 73 (1973) 4 (October), p.222-229.

Ronald Lockley, *Dear Islandman*. Llandysul, Gomer, 1996.

R.M. Lockley, *Dream Island. A Record of the Simple Life*. London, H.F. & G. Witherby, 1930.

R.M. Lockley, *Dream Island Days. A Record of the Simple Life*. London, H.F. & G. Witherby, 1943.

R.M. Lockley, *The Golden Year*. London, Readers Union / H.F. & G. Witherby, 1950 (1948[1]).

R.M. Lockley, *I Know an Island*. London, George G. Harrap, 1947 (1938[1]).

R.M. Lockley, *Inland Farm*. London, H.F. & G. Witherby, 1943.

Ronald Lockley, *The Island*. London etc., White Lion, 1975 (1969[1]).

Ronald Lockley, *Myself When Young. The Making of a Naturalist*. London, Deutsch, 1979.

R.M. Lockley, *Shearwaters*. London, J.M. Dent & Sons, 1947 (1942[1]).

R.M. Lockley, *The Way to an Island*. London, J.M. Dent & Sons, 1941.

R.M. Lockley, 'We Live Alone, and Like it – on an Island.' In: *The National Geographic Magazine* 74 (1938) 2 (August), p.252-278.

Douglas Martin, 'Ronald Lockley, of Rabbit Fame, Dies at 96.' In: *The New York Times*, 24 April 2000.

Margaret Morse Nice, 'The Eighth International Ornithological Congress.' In: *Bird Banding. Journal of Field Ornithology* 6 (1935) 1 (January), p.29-31.

Crossing the Divide

Kenneth Taylor

This is the Gap. The boundary between what has been described and the ground that few have mentioned. It cleaves the dark rocks from sky to sea, dividing the islands.

To one side is Hirta, core of St Kilda. It is an island whose layers of stories can seem to define the whole archipelago. Or overwhelm it. To the other is Dun. Once part of Hirta, its shape fills the view to the south when seen from a mile away in the village on the larger island.

At the Gap, the divide between the isles is narrow. But in the seven centuries during which many facets of St Kilda's landscape, human community and wildlife have been documented, Dun has been paid scant attention. If it appears at all, it is more as an afterthought to the main subject.

And that subject, often as not, is Hirta and the people who once lived there. By turns, I find Hirta's weight of words fascinating and exasperating. For whatever the tale told, there's an undertow in mind, a whisper of loss.

'But in the end, they had to abandon it, you know,' runs the refrain. 'It was on the 29th of August, 1930.' In years to come I will find myself re-telling the story of the evacuation to those keen to listen, whether here, on Britain's most remote island group, or on the mainland, whose Atlantic rim sits out of sight, a hundred miles away, over the eastern horizon. And sometimes I hate myself for it, because this is not the story I want to tell.

Yet, viewed with knowledge of past events, each old building, boundary, storehouse and wall on Hirta can seem to bear the imprint of loss. The way stones are aligned in a dyke; the wood rough-sawn and fitted as a door; how yellow iris crowds the wet hollows of former fields: all have that extra meaning.

It would take an unusual mind not to feel the pressure of the past here. So in some ways, the prod of it comes as no surprise on my first visit in 1976. What I don't expect, after riding the stomach-tugging rollercoaster of ocean for so long to reach here, is that Hirta could be so crowded. On this side, at least, where the curve of old houses in the one 'street' faces down to Village Bay, there's a clutter of buildings just beyond. The army base draws the eye, with its rectangular accommodation blocks, battleship grey, and the huge lump of a power station, its smoke stack thrusting a grimy finger to the Hebridean sky.

When I arrive, a single bright planet is chasing the crescent moon above the silhouetted humps of islands, each one seeming colossal in the half-light near dawn. I can hear the distant calls of seabirds and the sound of surf against the lip of the bay. It feels a waking dream, and seems to fit with so much of what I've imagined about this place.

'It's a big steen; a big, fucking *steen,*' complains a fellow traveller in a strong Glasgow accent. Broad-shouldered and stocky, he's a professional diver, part of a group of contractors come here to work on the jetty beside the army camp. He's spent much of the voyage downing red cans of beer, while asking, repeatedly, if anyone feels sick. 'Do you want to go and see *Hughey?*' he inquires, almost retching the name to give mocking emphasis to its mimicry. I try, unsuccessfully, to ignore his questions, though for a while on deck, looking at the crags, sky and sea, I forget.

Now he's broken the reverie again. It would have happened in any case, soon enough. For as we near the beach beneath the village, preparing for the landing craft to open its bow doors and lower metal ramps onto the strand, I feel I'm being assaulted by different sights and sounds. The roar and revving of engines from heavyweight vehicles on land, the dazzle of jetty lights and headlights, announcements from the ship's tannoy, shouted commands, a sudden outburst of laughter.

Walking down the ramp, its metal clanging underfoot, then wobbling ashore, legs unsteady after eight hours of crossing from the Uists, I feel not elation, but a kind of bewilderment. Part is sleep-deprivation, but part is because the place doesn't fit what I'd pictured. Maybe I've more in common with the diver than I reckoned.

In the weeks to come that summer, and in others ahead, I slowly re-think Hirta, imagining afresh as I read from books in the old Factor's House that I share with other seasonal residents. The whitewashed, one-and-a-half storey house sits just beyond the eastern end of the old street, its simple elegance tempered by the sheep dung at its doorstep and the concrete toilet block that part-obscures its view of the bay. The Nature Conservancy Council warden and a shifting cast of people who, like me, have come to help with studies of St Kildan seabirds or geology, are its temporary inhabitants.

In time, I fill the other houses along the street with people described in old accounts, see the precise locations where well-known photographs have been taken or snippets of grainy black-and-white movie film shot, visit the rocks and wells that had special significance to the islanders. Here was the house where Norman Gillies, part-time postmaster and purveyor of postcards and knitted socks for tourists, had lived. Here, part-way up the hill behind the village, was a large, grey rock, *Clach a'Bhainne,* the Milking Stone. 'In olden times,' writes an antiquarian, 'it was the custom to pour part of the first spring milking into a hollow in this boulder as a libation to the god *Gruagach* and to ensure the fertility of their cattle.

'As soon as the milk was poured, they could hear the fairies underneath rattling their spoons.'

No cattle had remained on the island after the evacuation, and the road that now snakes its blacktop up the brae from the army camp to the shoulder of Mullach Sgar, giving access to radar domes, comes very close to the stone. Not the most auspicious of conditions for fairies, perhaps. But somehow, the thought of that pagan ceremony gives a different energy to the village area. It contrasts with the many accounts of how the villagers, from the 19th century onwards, had been shackled to the stark version of Presbyterianism which still grips parts of the Outer Hebrides.

So strict was local adherence to church ways that some observers claimed (in apparent seriousness) that even the villagers' animals had a certain piety. One such was John Kerr, who accompanied the Moderator of the United Free Church on a short visit in 1914. Not a sound was heard when they came ashore, he wrote: '... for in St Kilda, the Sabbath begins at 12 noon on Saturday, and the dogs, of which there are fully forty on the island of a mongrel collie type, do not bark on that day.'

The comment was risible, but I warm to the notion of the motley bunch of dogs, whether god-fearing or not. It gives a vigour to the imagining of the place, as if some of the stiffness of a received idea of heritage has been relaxed. It is the same with thoughts of Finlay MacQueen, perhaps the most famous of all St Kilda's renowned cragsmen and bird catchers. Those come, not from notions of Finlay as a young man, but from descriptions of him when he returned for a summer visit, eight years after the evacuation.

The writer, Robert Atkinson, eloquent chronicler of visits to Scotland's outermost isles in the 1930s and 1940s, joined Finlay, Neil Gillies and Mrs Gillies during part of their stay. Finlay showed Robert how to snare puffins with a noose of horsehair, stiffened with a gannet quill and suspended from the end of a bamboo pole. Mrs Gillies was keen to collect 'crotal' – grey lichen that yields the red-brown dye for Harris tweed – by scraping it from the rocks with an old hoe. Sometimes Finlay would join her in the crotal gathering.

'Finlay came up on his broad bare feet with the well-spread toes; he carried a fowling rod, opera glasses, a sack and a coil of rope,' writes Atkinson.

'He walked slightly bow-legged with a long, swinging stride: as sure-footed as the sheep. He and Mrs Gillies were both nearer eighty than seventy; they climbed a thousand feet from the village, spent all day at the crotal, descended and thought nothing of it.'

Such are the characters, both human and animal, with which I populate the village and its surrounds. I visualize them as I walk, hearing, as these folk would once have done, the whinnying sound of snipe displaying over the meadows and the *chack-chack-chack* alarm calls of wheatears from the stonework. And looking across the bay, I see the outline of another place entirely; the place whose shape would have been as much a part of their mental picture of home as it is central to my own time here.

Dun rears from the sea, rising to nearly six hundred feet at a ragged shark fin of summit and stretching a huge breakwater along the southern edge of Village Bay. From the nearest point on Hirta, the distance to it could be crossed in a pebble's throw. But the gulf is treacherous.

At almost any time of day or night, sea fills the channel between the islands. Rocks, slick with weed and algal slime, protrude at low tide, all but the largest covered in white-streaked water at the tide's swell.

And when south-westerly gales pile on the Atlantic pressure, as they can do in any month here, the passage explodes with spray. Shattered to a billion gobbets, one blast of wind-driven sea can cannon fifty feet to skyward, filling the divide before bursting out against the waters of the bay.

This is the Gap. Its features and dangers have been enough

to dissuade most people, since the departure of the islanders, from attempting its challenge. The St Kildans once used Dun as pasture for rams and as a place to catch puffins to add to their larders of seabird meat. But I reckon that even they didn't view Dun as reliable of access. Hirta is peppered with drystone storage structures – 'cleits', as the old villagers called them – where ropes, peat, grain, potatoes or carcasses, including harvested birds, could be kept dry and wind-cooled. But Dun has no such buildings. Their absence, relatively close to the village, is telling.

Every year, a few groups make a crossing of the bay by outboard-powered inflatable to brave a landing on the slippery rocks of Dun's bayward edge. The Gap is not an option. So, often as not, Dun remains as a backdrop to life in and around the village; fairly close, yet unattainable.

But for a few summers, for a handful of people, the Gap can be tackled and Dun explored for more than a few hours at a time. A modified form of a 'Tyrolean Traverse' is the key to bridging the chasm. This mountaineering technique can be used to cross an obstacle (including free space) by hanging from a rope anchored tightly between two points. Seabird researcher, Mike Harris, who has invited me here to help with his work, and his regular assistant, Stuart Murray (a climber) have rigged a cable of twisted steel wire across the divide. A block and tackle sits on the cable, from which ropes splay down to support a swing seat, held within an old lifebelt ring.

A continuous loop of thin rope runs within reach from the seat assembly to roller blocks fixed on each side of the Gap. By hauling on one side of the loop, either single-handed or with help from someone on land, you can move the seat forward. In calm weather, with little wind and a helpful companion to share the heave, the contraption can speed across parts of the chasm. For a few seconds, it can feel like flying.

Stuart, already over on the Dun side of the Gap, helps to power my first flight, then shows me where to clamber up the rock to gain the turf of the island. 'Well, my loon,' he says, in measured Aberdeenshire tones, 'I wonder what the puffin psychologist will make of Dun?'

In the hours that follow, we move slowly along the island, feet scrunching through a lushness of sorrel and other plants whose growth is boosted by a rain of guano from Dun's breeding seabirds. This place has one of the largest congregations of seabirds in the whole of Britain, but at first, the plants are more to the fore than the birds. A few great black-backed gulls make curt warning calls as we pass their nests at the island edge, and an occasional fulmar glides above, stiff-winged. But it is the glossy sheen of the sorrel that catches the eye, the absence of puffins that seems intriguing.

'We call this the Sparse,' says Stuart. 'The puffin burrows can be quite far apart here, and the birds don't seem to spend very much time standing ashore in groups.'

We push beyond the Sparse, crossing a bridge of land where the sea has scooped deep into the island's south-west side and bitten a smaller chunk from its opposite flank. Masses of sea campion, each white flower backed by a balloon-like swelling, as if caught in mid-trumpet, froth down the slopes that rise both behind and beyond us.

Above, puffins swirl, flying out and back and out again from the edge of the summit slope that now rises just ahead. There are hundreds in the air at any one time, many more in groups on large tussocks and on flat-topped rocks. In the bay below, thousands stipple the blue-grey water, where they sit and preen, sleep or socialize before making a move from sea to land.

I've never before seen so many puffins together, nor been able to visualize the immensity of such a colony. 'This is the Dense,' says Stuart, further emphasising, with something approaching pride in his voice, the impressive contrast between different parts of the puffinry.

As we move up the summit slope, our progress is slow. This is not simply because of the steepness, which sometimes requires us to use handholds before rising further, but because the whole surface is lumpy with alternating tussocks and hollows. Put too much strain on a tussock, with boot or hand, and it can dislodge. A tumbling fall, sliding down to where the grass and campion overhang the cliffs, could be a fast-track to oblivion here.

The physical challenges and the slight frisson of danger combine to make me focus on the nuances of the ground. The shadow of a puffin burrow entrance, how a clump of grass is aligned, the feeling of soil crumbling under boot or staying firm, the way a nearby fulmar eyes me: already Dun is coaxing me to an awareness of it in the present moment. I have no stories in mind as I move up its sunlit face, no baggage of preconceptions.

And when we reach the summit and pause, the sense of interest in what is near at hand has become much greater than what can be described, from prior knowledge, in the wider view. Across the bay, I can discern each house in the village, each cleit, if I choose to do so. But here, there are other priorities. Big, daisy-like flowers of scentless mayweed stud the greenery near the summit. White-petalled and yellow-hearted, they make a carpet of stars beneath us.

I've never before seen such a show of pattern and colour on a hilltop. I'm struck by both the otherness and the intimacy of Dun, as if each feature of the island is coaxing me to experience it with a freshness I'd almost forgotten how to savour.

When Stuart begins to name features on the islands, I realize that each applies to land and landmarks set apart from the island we now occupy. Dun seems to have very few names that have stuck, over the millennia since Neolithic people first came to St Kilda.

Returning, through that summer and two more to follow, I relish Dun's lack of names. Somehow, their relative absence makes it easier to sense aspects of life that seem detached from human involvement. I perceive the island in an utterly different way from its near neighbour. For there is no obvious, inherited sub-text to this place, just the fascination of the here and now.

I do have my own purpose in repeated visits to Dun, often as the only person on its whole, bird-thronged bulk. My aim is to learn about aspects of how puffins organize their lives in such a large colony and how they try to avoid falling prey to great black-backed gulls. But that too is new, with little scientific data, collected by others, to draw on to inform my own explorations. To discover anything fresh, I must be alert for signs for which there is no existing guidebook.

And the island helps me to do it. Again and again, its subtleties of shape, texture, smell and sound help me to focus on the moment. In turn, that helps me to see patterns in the whirling flocks, make scientific sense of their rhythms and turns.

But sometimes, just sometimes, the island coaxes me to let go of those ways of describing the life here, new though they are, and simply revel in its wildness. When I climb down above a sea cave and the sound of singing rises, part howl, part mellifluous, from unseen seals, I hear it. When a gull lifts to the sky, soaring above the wheeling puffins and its outline, though small, becomes the epicentre of the whole, wide panorama, I sense it. When the spent, translucent flowerheads of sea pinks are sparked by the evening sun to make a field of tiny lights as I walk back along the island, I can feel it.

And though I cannot predict when these moments of connection will happen, I know that this island is making me more open to them. In decades to come, I will encounter such feelings in many other places, always unexpected, yet familiar, like a tingle of hairs at a lover's touch.

Right now it is Dun that is coaxing me to let go. I watch a gull fly near and then settle, calmly, to look out at the waters of the bay. And a stillness fills me. I am seeing the gull, the circling birds, the rocks and sea as if a rain shower has been followed by bright sun. Each aspect has a clarity that is both visual and more than visual.

Later, when I reach the edge of the island and grasp the ropes to begin the haul, something of that feeling remains. I pull, and the apparatus swings me out over the chasm.

Hirta looms. Dun is behind. But I am carrying part of it with me.

This is the Gap.

Explorations in a Legendary Landscape

Michelle Cotter

I stand in dazzling sunshine on the summit Knocknarea, with my back to the famous cairn of stones known as *Miosgan Maedhbha* (Maeve's Cairn) taking photographs of Sligo Bay and the Dartry Mountains, the spectacular limestone plateau North of Sligo Bay. On such a cloudless day the view is stunning. I observe the expanse of the Dartry range from Benbulben to Kings Mountain and Truskmore, Sligo's highest mountain. I look eastwards over Glencar and into County Leitrim. Sligo has been made immortal in the poetry and folklore of W. B. Yeats, and in the paintings of his brother Jack. In the shadow of Benbulben lies the poet himself, removed posthumously from France according to his last request, to be laid in Drumcliffe churchyard.

This dramatic landscape of weathered limestone cliffs, glacial valleys, waterfalls, peat bogs and sheep trails retains, even today, traces of the old folk tales, myths and supernatural happenings which inspired Yeats and many others. Of each of the individual mountains, Benbulben is probably the most renowned, though the name 'Benbulben' is used frequently to indicate the entire Dartry Range. As I gaze across Sligo Bay from where I stand on Knocknarea I am aware that, though I could name each peak, plateau and cairn on the horizon in any direction and identify every contour of it on an Ordnance Survey map, this is a place that also defies definition. The legendary landscape of Sligo that is so frequently represented in literature and the visual arts is also a place touched by controversy: conflicting values, aesthetics and debates over land use and access. My attempt to get to know this place has challenged my perception in ways I could not have imagined.

At the foot of these immutable, seductive heights Sligo is a thriving, populous place. Sligo City's narrow muddle of streets is a constant bustle of locals and tourists, its outlying towns also. In spite of this constant flow of human activity the thing that has captivated me about Sligo since my very early childhood, unfailingly, is its mountainscape. I recall the summer journeys west from Dublin; catching a glimpse of Benbulben thrust upwards from the sea like an ancient and impenetrable curtain wall, the granite Ox Mountains like the bunched fists of some mythical warrior; Slieve Da Ean, the mount of the two birds, Killery, Carin's Hill, Knocknarea – names that still conjure up magical and dark tales. The mountainscape of Sligo has dominated the collective consciousness and imagination of all who live and pass through here.

In one version of *Scéal Toraiocht Diarmaid agus Gráinne* (The Pursuit of Diarmaid and Grainne), the Fenian cycle legend most associated with this area, Diarmaid outwitted his enemy Fionn Mac Cumhaill while hiding in the mountains. He and Gráinne were hiding in a cave in Benbulben summit from which there was an underground passage out to the sea at Moneygold. An old woman lived there who, it was believed, never told a lie, and Diarmaid sought her advice. The old woman told him to fill his bag with sand from the beach at Moneygold, take it with him to the mountain top and spread it on the ground beneath himself and Gráinne when they slept. She told him that each time they left the cave for the seashore, he should fill his bag with mountain heather and spread it out beneath them on the sand. When Fionn Mac Cumhaill arrived at the summit of Benbulben and could see no trace of his foe, he sought out this woman who never lied and asked her where the couple were hiding. She replied that they were lying on the sand. He went down to the seashore at Moneygold but could find no trace of Diarmaid and Grainne. Fionn asked the old woman the following day and she replied; 'they lie on the heather', whereupon he climbed up Benbulben Mountain and still could not find them.[1]

What I find interesting in this tale is how the old woman used the *terrain* to conceal the lovers and to confuse Fionn Mac Cumhaill, how she cleverly overlayed the adjacent topographies of mountain and seashore in her replies. Legend or no, it suggests to me the interdependence between the upland and maritime communities in this part of Sligo over the ages.

Driving out towards Mullaghmore, about ten miles North of Sligo town, I can see the scar of disused limestone quarries flanking the mountains. The pier at Mullaghmore harbour was constructed from this quarried stone in the last century. I can imagine how the lower fields would have been spread with seaweed, how farmers and fishermen traded and negotiated, I think of the long-abandoned railway that ran from the barytes mines in Glencarberry to Mullaghmore harbour for transportation to Sligo.

Nowadays even fishing has been scaled down dramatically in these parts – a casualty of Ireland's economic 'development'. Tourism is now a major source of income in North Sligo, and many of the picturesque white bungalows dotted along the Donegal road are only seasonally occupied. The livelihoods and demographies of these communities have changed, but the memory of the past is locked fast into earth and stone, a great reservoir of stories and experiences.

When I come out here it is as if the ground shifts beneath my feet, past and present blur in my perception. Whether walking on the sand or the heather I am absorbed in the perennial drama

[1] From The Schools Manuscript Collection 1938, University College Dublin: Delargy Centre for Irish Folklore and the National Folklore Collection..

of coast and mountain simultaneously.

What makes mountains so special? I discussed this with locally based archaeologist Stefan Bergh, who has excavated the megalithic burial complex at Carrowmore, south of Sligo Bay. He suggested that it is the elevation and visibility of mountains that commands attention and authority; their proximity to the heavens, their isolation – the fact that a mountain is the most visible feature on any horizon, and yet the most obscure. Nobody can see what's going on at the top. It is difficult to get up there. Mountains are mysterious. He pointed out that in Ireland, in fact all over the world, the greatest monumental sites are built on elevated ground.

Though there are no cairns or the likes on the Dartry Plateau; south of the Garavogue River Knocknarea boasts the impressive *Miosgan Maebha,* over 20m high; unexcavated but comparatively dated to about 2,000 BC. Local folklore claims that this is the final resting place of Maeve, the warrior queen of Connaught. Smaller cairns dating from this period are situated on Cairn's hill and on the hill tops of Southern Sligo at Carrowkeel and Kesh Corran. The Dartry plateau, however, has accrued a wealth of heritage that is immaterial: legends, folk tales and practices.

Local lore has a tendency to personify these mountains or to speak of them in terms of the human body or that of an animal. The Gleniff Valley is often referred to as the 'Heels' of Benbulben and Benwiskin; Benbulben's lower slopes as 'Giant's Feet' in the Duff River. Benbulben is often associated with the famous boar of *Sceal na Toraiochta; Torc Bhinne Gulban.* It is interesting to observe the cloud formations on the lower slopes – a short stretch of the imagination and you have the impression of a boar, giant horses or other fantastical beings. The shape of the plateau summit suggests that something inhabits or moves around on the mountaintop.

University College Dublin's Centre for Irish Folklore houses the marvellous 'School's Collection' of manuscripts; accounts of folk tales and practices collected by schoolchildren from their elders throughout Ireland during the 1930s. Here I find the tale of a ferocious wild cat who lived in a ruined fort on Benbulben mountain, and I read about the black hound of Grúcan na Cú. Another account describes Benbulben as a 'great giant overlooking the sea' and lists the following place names upon the mountains:

> *Suidhe Finn (the Seat of Finn) Leaba Diarmad agus Gráinne (the Bed/Grave of Diarmad and Grainne), Crip-Rock, Míne (smoothness), Poll Ciúin (the Quiet Hole), King's Mountain, The Bush, Andy's Peak, The One River, The Three Rivers and The Love Rock.*[2]

Some of these are purely descriptive (*Míne,* The Three Rivers etc.) while others are historical or mythologically associated. I have been curious to locate these names in the present, to see if they have persisted in local memory beyond the 1930s. There are many accounts of holy wells and fairy forts in the general environs, which tend to draw in the lore of the mountains.

Local people defer to the mountains when speaking of the weather. If Benbulben looks far away, for example, it is a sign of good weather. If the sheep are clearly visible in the slopes it is a sign of bad weather. If the mountain looms close it is also a bad sign. If the hole in the mountainside known as Poll Gorm (the Blue Hole) looks green at sunset, fine weather is to be expected, bad weather if it looks black. Mist is referred to as 'Benbulben wearing his white cap'.[3]

---

[2] From The Schools Manuscript Collection 1938, S155-157: University College Dublin: Delargy Centre for Irish Folklore and the National Folklore Collection.

[3] Ibid: S157.

The traditions of representation and metaphor in the Dartry Mountains area long predate the poetry and prose of W. B. Yeats, who had a fascination with the place. What Yeats achieved was to endorse a romantic vision of landscape and the Sublime and fix it definitively in this space in County Sligo. It is this vision that is nurtured in Sligo Tourism (amongst others) and that presents this area as a scenic attraction.

In 1977 Foras Forbartha (The Irish National Institute of Physical Planning and Construction Research) included the Dartry Mountains in its *Inventory of Outstanding Landscapes in Ireland,* describing the terrain as follows:

> *'Mesa-like landform with high blocks of peat-covered horizontal limestone surrounded by sheer cliffs and scree slopes. Slipped cliff sections stand above some of the deep valleys, which are, now filled with moraine-dammed lakes (Glendale and Glencar Loughs.) Hazel scrub is widespread and Lough Gill in the south is wooded extensively. Bays, Islands and peninsulas give it an intimate feeling unlike the large Lough Melvin in the north, which is rather featureless except for some large islands. The lumpy hills of gneiss in the south are a notable contrast in shape. High botanical, ecological and zoological interest.'*

Though a geological/ecological description of terrain, the use of such terms as 'intimate' and 'featureless' demonstrate how we are taught to value and receive landscape. Our eyes are trained to look for the arresting feature, our emotions to respond in a certain way. Terence O'Rourke's History of Sligo Town and County describes the Gleniff Valley as:

> *'A huge grotto ... spacious apartments to the right and left as you enter, the lofty gallery in front and the corridors or passages here and there, the interior has*

the features of some lordly mansion or some great cathedral of the Middle Ages picturesquely vaulted and grounded in genuine, solid stone.'[4]

Here are two very different responses to the physical terrain of Sligo both attempting to capture the aesthetic experience of the place. O'Rourke's response is euphemistic and figurative, the Foras Forbartha piece is descriptive. Both extracts romanticise the landscape – even if unconsciously.

Yeats' mountains were populated by supernatural beings, ancient heroes and fairies, but his vision is a romantic representation, which tends to ignore the living community of these landscapes. Perhaps this is one of the reasons that to this day, people and 'scenery' can be incompatible. The landscape of the Dartry Mountains may be sparsely populated compared to the lower reaches of Sligo, but it is not devoid of human activity. Tourism sells the aesthetic experience of sightseeing and walking in an unspoilt isolated landscape, visualising it as the poet or the painter might. Somewhere between aesthetics and the physical terrain is the living heritage of the rural community: their relationship to their environment through the ages. A recent and ongoing debate between local farmers and visiting hill walkers has brought these issues to the fore.

Benbulben and the rest of the Dartry Plateau have been listed in tourist publications as a *recreational* landscape. It is possible to drive the 'Boar of Benbulben tour', which overlaps with much of the Yeats Country scenic drive (160 km)[5]. However, it has come to light that the appropriation of

---

[4] O'Rourke: 1986: Vol I:514.

[5] These tour routes are illustrated in a publication entitled 'Sligo, Land of Heart's Desire: Driving Tours and Short Walks' produced by several regional and state bodies in co-operation: the Lough Arrow Research Project with FAS, Sligo Leader Partnership and Northwest Tourism.

the mountain landscape for recreational purposes has angered many local communities who make a living off the same land. In some cases where lands are privately owned, Tourist organisations have delineated walking routes without asking permission. Where Irish Tourist Board signage exists in fields (to indicate a monument or object of historical interest) there is a certain right of way for tourists; however, no such signposts apply in the case of 'scenery', which is almost impossible to define by a set of criteria.

About ten years ago the case of a North Sligo farmer made the headlines of the national newspapers. A tourist guide had mapped a public walking route to the summit of Benbulben through his lands, without his permission or foreknowledge. The farmer was taken to court to defend his attack on the tourists who were walking on his property. What ensued was a complex web of accusations and claims. In the end he was fined, but other farmers in the Gleniff Valley raised money for him as a gesture of solidarity. Farmers in Gleniff claimed that hill walkers (who frequently have dogs) disturb their sheep and often lead to their being frightened over the edge of the cliffs and killed. It was a long and bitter conflict which divided community and recreational visitors according to their different ways of seeing and being in the landscape; the desire to 'roam the wilderness' and those making a living from the land. I remember being deeply conflicted myself. I had recently moved into a rural community to research the relationship between people and a place of archaeological value, where issues of land use and access were often fraught. On the other hand, as a hill walker, I could not imagine a legislation that would forbid or restrict access to the Sligo hills.

As I suggested, the Sligo mountainscape inspires opinion and ideas that often conflict or contradict one another. Debates over access arise time and time again, as do conflicts of interest over rural development and tourist marketing. After a time the contentious issues of the present evolve into tales of the past. I have spent time studying and researching this landscape in every way, but somehow, for me, its innate mystery is never compromised by economics or politics, the sublime beauty of this place never marred by critique. Thinking again of Diarmaid and Grainne's mythical escape to Benbulben I recognise this mountain terrain as a kind of benevolent sanctuary where it is possible to simply enjoy the experience.

Bibliography

An Foras Forbartha. 1977. *Inventory of Outstanding Landscapes in Ireland*. Dublin.

Jeffares, A. Norman (ed.)1980. *Yeats, Sligo and Ireland: Essays to mark the 21st Yeats International Summer School*. Gerrards Cross: Colin Smythe.

O'Rourke, Terence. 1986. *History of Sligo Town and County.* Sligo: Dodd's Antiquarian Books.

The Schools Manuscript Collection 1938, S155-157, University College Dublin: Delargy Centre for Irish Folklore and the National Folklore Collection.

Wild Life on Braighlinne

Mandy Haggith

I have the privilege of living in Scotland's 'wild west', a marvellous land, buffeted continuously by the Atlantic, storm-sculpted and sparsely populated. I inhabit a croft called Braighlinne. The saying goes that a croft is a small piece of land surrounded by a large piece of legislation. In the case of Braighlinne, where I live with Bill, it is an 11-hectare patch of woodland with a hole in the middle. Inside the hole is a house, where Duncan the previous crofter lived much of his life. It is a typical 1920s crofthouse, one and a half storeys of white-painted stone, with slate roof and poky windows. After Duncan died in the early 1990s, the house site was 'decrofted', a legal procedure to remove it from the clutches of the legislation that binds the remainder of the land, so that the building and its garden could be freely traded on the open market. Since then various people have bought and sold the house, used now only as a holiday home, and it has become snazzier and less affordable with every occupant. Meanwhile Bill and I occupy the surrounding land, unhoused and, by definition therefore, not very domesticated.

We have a lifestyle that is closer to the natural world than we could achieve if we inhabited a stone-walled, multi-roomed structure. Instead of a house, we have two twelve-foot caravans, four sheds and an upturned boat, dotted about the croft. Each has a distinct function (bath, bed, kitchen, storage etc). The croft is thus effectively a very large, outdoor dwelling place with six indoor rooms and a couple of lean-tos. One visitor described it as 'an exploded house', another as 'radically detached'. Bill calls it our '11-hectare house', and claims to have the biggest home in the land.

Our adoption of a simplicity principle means that we don't have a lot of the things many people seem to view as essential to twenty-first-century domestic life, such as flush toilet, shower, oven, fridge, washing machine and television. We don't have mains electricity. We don't have a mortgage, insurance or proper jobs. But we do have 11 hectares of paradise, complete with the best bathroom in the world, a wooden studio where I do freelance writing and environmental activism thanks to wireless broadband (powered by wind and sun) and a bed with a lochside view of curlews, black-throated divers, otters and seals.

❧ ❧ ❧

On a late winter morning, in cold grey drizzle, I stroll out onto the wildest part of the croft: Rhoin an Oba, 'point in the bay', a foot-shaped rocky promontory out into Loch Roe. The tide changes the water level by five metres or more, so the Rhoin shrinks and grows to a twice-daily pulse, disintegrating into an archipelago of islands as the tide comes in, then reconstituting itself into unity as the sea drops away.

At first there does not seem to be much going on, but gradually the residents reveal themselves. A pair of hooded crows scavenges among seaweed on the south shore of the loch. They give a hostile caw, perhaps to me, perhaps to the black-backed gull that soars over, heading east, coasting on the stiff south-westerly breeze. Down the otter track, on bracken flattened by smoothing feet, the old wooden dinghy lies, holed, waiting to be upended as a make-shift shelter, at least until a storm rolls it back over again. A rock pipit flits rock to rock to rock as I scramble on. Six small rowans tremble, stark brown against the pewter loch, up to their thighs in ragged heather. An unseaworthy knot of honeysuckle is already putting leaves out. A curlew races by, heading east, letting the wind hurtle it along. Three mergansers fly in, splash to a halt and bounce on the waves. A herring gull swerves in and over me, giving me the eye.

Right out to the point, scrub birch and willow hunker in the teeth of the wind. On the rock, scurvy grass and stonecrop have found footholds. Between them is lichen; an abstract medley of colour. I am too ignorant to name them all. They are green, white, orange, wispy, baubled, crusty, smooth, some like maps, some like a peeling sunburned skin. Altogether magnificent.

Today there are seven seals visible in Loch Roe, all pretty-faced and inappropriately named common seals, which are far less common than the bigger greys. Three pairs lounge about like big lead-coloured slugs on the chocolate-brown seaweed fringe around the biggest skerry. In the inlet between the closest island and the shore is another. It hangs in the water, nose pointing skywards. It appears to have an expression of ecstasy on its puppy-face. I have often snorkelled there and imagine the seal rubbing itself in the rubbery-lace bladderwrack. It turns to look at me, eyes soft, wet and curious. It makes an approach, as if in greeting, then swims towards the reef in the middle of the loch, its back breaking the surface in a regular wave motion. Often the seals curve right out of the water as they swim, like porpoises. It snorts and humps itself onto the island, wriggling up to the highest point, where it bends upwards in a banana shape before slumping with a satisfied 'hmf' into a position of utter relaxation. The tide is fairly low and still falling: an ideal time to grab a soft weedy rock to snooze on for a few hours.

Who else is out here? A heron has been watching my advance and takes off with a squawk. Pools harbour periwinkles and limpets, barnacles and jelly anemones. There are tell-tale shells, spelling out the menu of otter feasts: mussels and velvet crab. Millions of shell shards make mosaics in fissures, so orderly they appear engineered, a flamboyant artwork of shell-fish grouting. There is such richness of texture here in miniature. I think of

Robert Macfarlane, seeking the enlightenment of wildness on a Sutherland mountain and finding it in the tiny natural worlds inhabiting cracks in rock. He could have found it here too.

I peer into a little pool at the edge of the furthermost rock. Barnacles. A white periwinkle. Pebbles stained red and green by algae. When I look up there – there! just a few metres away! – is a black-throated diver, grace in feathered form. It dives the perfect dive all other birds strive towards but fail to achieve. So different from the cormorant, which jumps up and ducks under, or the dab chick, which simply vanishes, the diver flows down into the water. It is under a long time, several minutes, emerging way across the loch. It is up only for a few seconds, then does that dive again.

The breeze weaves the loch surface to a shiny grey corduroy. The two crows chase each other and the gull flits away westwards. I slither back up to dry land and retrace mindful steps across the psychedelic lichens.

❦ ❦ ❦

Braighlinne contains a remarkable mixture of habitats. About half is native woodland, and most of the rest is boggy or heathery, with some craggy spots by the shore, and even a little salt marsh. Although compared with much of the rest of Scotland this seems like a place where nature is strong, thousands of years of human habitation have left their mark. The woods have been modified by burning and grazing. There are a few tumbled ruins, a couple of small patches that have been cultivated in times long past and a flattish area where a stream has been deepened to drain and improve pasture.

Bill got the croft in the early 1990s, and ever since has managed it with the aim of restoring the ecosystems to something closer to their wild state. In practice, this means that we largely leave nature to take its course. Some people think that this is not 'real crofting'. Yet 'crofter forestry' is a perfectly legal land-use and for most of the past two decades, this rewilding effort on Braighlinne has been sanctioned as part of a formal agreement with the Scottish Forestry Commission, which encourages woodland regeneration on suitable land.

An unsympathetic neighbour, who has since moved away, once complained that we were letting bracken, rushes and trees grow unchecked. When we tried to explain that this was not mere neglect, but a conscious and deliberate strategy to encourage wild animals and birds, our neighbour shrieked, 'The only wildlife here is you!' She was wrong, of course, but we were secretly pleased that our efforts to become less domesticated were being recognised.

I turn east, along the shore, into the woods. Birch, rowan, aspen and willow grow right down to the high-tide line, shrunken and twisted by constant salt-wind stress. The undergrowth is at its minimum. Bracken is a bronze collapse, but there is plenty of green still: wood-sage, plantain, the little antlers of blaeberry, glossy hard fern, heathers and ling, with their blond seed-bobbles. Sphagnum mosses cover a spectrum of colour from copper pink through gold to lime. Two struggling hollies are cropped into bushes by deer – our presence here has some deterrent effect, but it is limited. This is their place too. I wonder how they can bear the prickles in their mouths, but clearly the succulent leaves are worth suffering for.

Crouched behind a rocky rise, a multi-stemmed oak tree – who knows how ancient? – still retains some of its leaves, like crumpled brown envelopes. The path winds through the wiggly woods to the stream, which is chortling today. Through gaps in the trees, the seal watches my slow progress.

A branch of a birch has been torn off in a recent storm, and

I shift it to the side of the path. There is almost as much dead wood here as living and I wonder if that proportion is growing as storminess increases. Many birch stems are scorched corpses, but new growth sprouts from their bases, a natural coppicing performed by the wind. The best chanterelles grow here, among the ragged birches, in summertime. An aspen stands, implausibly straight and tall, on the seaward edge. Around a spreading willow there are red deer droppings. Up in the canopy there is the sound of a bird tap-tapping a shell, but when I look up, I see it is no winged creature, just two dead aspen leaves, shrunken and desiccated, but still clapping applause with the wind, as aspens do.

The path rises to the edge of a crag overlooking a sheltered cove. A rope hangs down the cliff, and as I abseil down between a tangle of honeysuckle, bramble, laminaria lichens and aspen suckers, I startle three mallards who fly low over the loch to the safety of the south shore.

This is Kelvin Grove, called in jest after the posh Glasgow area, from which it could not be more different. It is a grove of aspen trees, ranged like muscular ballet dancers around a rocky stage. This place, inaccessible as it is, has been used by people in the past, perhaps for thousands of years. Stones have been cleared for easy passage of a boat, and heaped into a dyke for shelter. Our dinghy is tied here, wintering. An earlier boat rotted away here, sometime in the first half of the twentieth century, leaving only its rusted Kelvin engine, eaten away a little more by every tide. Hence the name.

Rock and washed-up seaweed are spattered with white guano. I wrote a haiku here:

> under the aspen
> where the heron shits
> – the first primrose

Unfortunately, this beautiful sheltered inlet acts as a magnet for plastic. A winter's worth of bags, crates and bottles has accumulated. It's not true what they say, 'there's no such place as away'. Away is here. The stuff tossed there all seems to come to Loch Roe, washed in by storms, by inexorable westerly winds and currents: buckets and bottles, fish boxes and rope, ketchup pots and margarine tubs, buoys and fenders and bits of old boats, bottle tops and bin bags, carriers and cans. It's all here. We go 'wombling' every year, dragging out sack after sack, stuffed with all this detritus, but we wait until spring when our disgust for all this human rubbish can be tempered by the delight of birdsong, primroses, scurvy grass and thrift. Today I simply chant my favourite Shetlandic signpost – dinna chuck bruck – until my temper cools.

Out in the loch, the black-throated diver croons its heart-rending loon song.

Wildness is a term to be used carefully in Scotland. There is little really wild land here, at least not in the objective sense of land that is untrammelled by human activity. But there are places that feel wild, if you are willing to allow that wildness is at least partly a subjective phenomenon, or a way of describing a relationship between a place and a person. Even in the objective sense, wildness is not an all-or-nothing concept; it's a spectrum from one extreme of the deep Arctic, to small corners of urban waste ground where wild life clings, and a land's position on this spectrum is not fixed. Just as the incursion of a road into pristine forest can reduce its wildness, so also, wildness can increase, a place can regain wild character, nature can strengthen its hold, even here in Scotland. So too, a person can move counter to the mainstream urban currents of consumer culture, in search of an earthier way of being. For the past decade I have tried to achieve some form of 'rewilding' of both myself and the land I dwell on, seeking to understand how people and land can develop their wild natures together.

Apart from wombling, what else does rewilding mean in practice? Bill and I mostly let plants grow and wildlife do their own thing, whatever that might be. We have no livestock and the croft is fenced to keep sheep, cattle and horses out while being permeable to wild animals, including deer. Apart from a small patch of willow, herbs and vegetables, we do not till the ground. We use no chemicals. We do not burn. We do not cut trees. We do not collect deadwood. We try to minimise our impact on the croft and live as lightly as possible.

The result of more than a decade of this regime is that the pasture has been invaded by bracken and rushes, it is host to masses of tall flowering herbs such as skullcap, sneezewort, meadowsweet, valerian and knapweed, and gradually bigger plants like brambles and willows are turning some of it to scrub. The heather is deep, loose and straggly. The drainage ditches are starting to clog up with vegetation. The native woodland is spreading. The croft is, superficially at least, becoming wilder.

However, all of our stipulations are problematic to some extent. Deer are constantly attacking the young trees and left to their own devices they would certainly curtail the woodland's regeneration. They have no natural predators here; all the big native carnivores that originally used to provide the natural balance in the ecosystem (wolf, bear and lynx) were exterminated in Scotland hundreds of years ago. So we actively try to disturb deer when they come on the croft. How forcefully we do this has varied over the past decade, from a polite request not to eat the trees, to a phone call to a neighbour with a gun. Most entertainingly perhaps, Bill spent a couple of years swearing vigorously at them at the top of his voice and I used to speculate that the neighbours and passing tourists may have suspected the onset of Tourette's syndrome. We clap a lot. We also use tree guards to protect some tree seedlings, particularly rowan and oak, which are browsed preferentially by roe deer.

Impatient with the process of natural seed dispersal, we have done what is termed 'enhancement planting', growing seed of nearby trees of species absent on the croft, namely ash, wild cherry and alder and of species that are numerically few, including oak, holly and elder. Should we also be taking active steps to block up drainage ditches, to re-wet the ground, like the bog restoration work in the Flow Country? Or should we resist the urge to keep intervening?

The presence of domestic livestock, and the active maintenance of pasture, created the conditions for some grassland plants that cannot survive the natural succession to scrub and woodland. We have already seen the disappearance of gentians, and the lesser butterfly orchids are in decline. Where they grew, burnet roses now thrive with their attendant black-and-scarlet moths. I am learning that rewilding does not necessarily mean an increase in biodiversity. Should we be worried about this, or is it better to feel a little humble, and accept that natural selection will not necessarily make the selection that I would choose?

Neighbouring crofters regularly (and one more often than most) set fire to heather in early spring to keep it short and better for grazing. We wonder what we would do if such a fire spread to Braighlinne. Would we fight it? Or is fire a natural process that would be followed by an interesting succession of regrowth?

One of the most difficult questions we face is what to do about windblown trees. The hurricane of 2005 uprooted several birches and willows. We stood two of them back up again, taking some limbs off, but the rest we left where they were, to rot or grow horizontally. The cut limbs became firewood, which raises an important dilemma. Other than thinnings around the garden, we do not cut wood on the croft, and we leave deadwood rather than gather it for burning, because it is such an important habitat for fungi, invertebrates and all the birds and other animals that eat them. It is also a store of carbon in the forest. However, this means that we need to import fuel for space and water heating. We burn some bottled gas and have a wood stove, so one of the impacts of our rewilding decision is our use of fossil fuel and wood from a nearby conifer plantation. Given that these both contribute to climate change, one of the strongest effects of which is an increase in severe weather events like hurricanes, the question of whether or not to burn wind-blown trees leaves us scratching our heads. Rewilding puts us into an eco-centric position, where the interests of protection of this ecosystem are put before the geo-centric need to think globally. Not for us the confident certainties of Thoreau.

⁂

Continuing my walk, I scramble out of Kelvin Grove among fallen boulders, trees growing improbably on and among them, towards the Uighe, the narrows where the water from Lochan Saile, which we all just call 'the middle loch', pours out into Loch Roe, at least some of the time. Sometimes it flows in the other direction, inland. It all depends on the tide. I hope I never cease to enjoy the wonder of living by a river that can flow upstream as well as down. For now it is pretending to be normal, flowing west towards the sea, babbling over weedy stones.

Back in the shelter of trees again, the water sounds are muffled by moss. It glows in the grey light, overhung by hazel catkins, which swell with each day that passes. Something, a badger by the look of it, has been digging under a rock, exposing roots and the dark, brown, rich soil of ancient woodland.

Turning north, I stroll inland under a birch twig lacework. In a boggy clearing, stunted trees give way to deep sphagnum moss, scruffy heather and grasses. The ground slops and squelches underfoot. In summer this is frog heaven and dragonfly paradise.

Back under trees again, a woodcock beats away at thunderous speed, looking as if it must batter itself senseless against a branch, but somehow zig-zagging unharmed out of the tangle of birch twigs. I hug my favourite rowan, a multi-stemmed marvel that has formed itself into a plait of fused trunks. The undergrowth here has been flattened by roe deer.

This small patch of woodland opens out to the largest clear area on the croft, probably once used as a hay meadow, but not within living memory. Here birches are regenerating with gusto, despite the wet ground, reclaiming it after years as pasture. At the edge are the kitchen-caravan, bath-shed, toolshed, polytunnel and garden.

❧❧❧

My tiny garden only provides a small fraction of the food that we eat, and thereby arises another paradox. I could undoubtedly grow more, but only by tilling more ground and introducing exotic species. Most of the food plants we enjoy are not native to Scotland, and to grow them successfully requires an ongoing struggle with the local wildlife, from the blackbirds too fat to fly from gorging themselves on redcurrants to the voles that systematically devour every bean seed I put in the ground, not forgetting the deer, who seem to like chomping apple trees even more than rowans. Even nature-friendly organic gardening is an intensive land-use that is anything but wild, yet by meeting more of our food needs on the croft we could reduce our footprint on the rest of the planet.

Part of the answer is to eat more wild food: making salads with weeds, foraging for mushrooms, picking berries, gathering seaweed. This gets me to the issue of how, as part of the rewilding experiment, we can become wilder in ourselves. There is no question that over the past decade I have become a lot less tame than I used to be.

My early land management thinking, shaped by a scientific and academic background, involved rigorous planning, schedules of actions, a detailed programme of monitoring and rules. These have mostly fallen by the wayside. Ten years ago we had a rule to keep to the paths. These days, we use a network of footways that have evolved to be the most efficient routes from one place to another, and these change from time to time as mud develops, or trees grow, and we bumble around wherever we need to go. Our decision-making about intervention on the croft has become ad-hoc and driven by events or need, rather than planned out. We only monitor if we will learn from it.

Our lifestyle is fairly 'wild'. We're off-grid and drink from the stream. We compost all our waste, including our 'humanure'. Because of our distributed home, we regularly encounter the other animals with whom we share this place. If I want a cup of tea, I must walk 250 metres from the studio to the kitchen-caravan tucked in the woods at the east side of the croft. In summer I'll pass five species of orchids with their attendant butterflies, and on winter evenings my torch light may pick out the eyes and white rumps of roe deer. Sometimes I'm in full waterproofs and wondering if I am more than a little mad. But at any time a sparrowhawk may low-fly past (just as, to shatter any growing sense of cosy closeness to nature, a military jet may gash over with its devastating roar, spewing fossil-fuel fumes and reminders of war). Every trip to the toilet, day or night, rain or fine, ice or midgies, is an opportunity for bumping into a shrew or an owl. Of course, because nowhere here is truly wild, there is nothing to be afraid of – no chance of stumbling on a boar or startling a lynx; at night there is no howl of wolf, no growl of bear. Yet still visitors say it feels like the wildest place they have ever been.

The croft is an endless source of images and ideas. Last night a storm roared in from wherever out there it had been brewing. I lay awake for hours in the dark, listening. The bed shed rattled and shook. The trees are flexible enough to withstand most of what the Atlantic Ocean brings in; they roar like a rock-stadium crowd all night, bucking and dancing, twisting and tossing. Then in the morning they're all innocence and calm, with just a scatter of twigs by way of a hangover. I too have weathered storms and I'm wiser for it.

Getting to know the wildlife here is a source of endless inspiration. Yesterday we stood gazing at a red deer hind in the woods, who stared back with a calm if questioning grace, her brown hide so nearly camouflaged against hazel stems and oak bark. This morning two little grebes dived with simultaneous vanishing acts then bobbed up just out of synch, making their way up the fast-flowing uighe down which the middle loch flows out into Loch Roe, at the eastern edge of the croft. There, last week, we watched an otter head out on a fishing expedition, weaving among seaweeds on the outgoing tide, lithe as a wet cat, intent on its hunting foray. Pine martens and foxes put signature droppings on the paths or just outside the caravan door. A weasel left footprints in the bath. The seals have grown accustomed to us and no longer jump off the skerries when we approach the shore. They teach me about tides and freedom, and make their way into my poems.

seals hunt and grunt
ignorant but blunt
no-one's instrument

One of the most meaningful aspects of my own rewilding has been the development of seasonal variation in behaviour. Some of these changes are weather-related, for example, in winter I strive to avoid working indoors on sunny days: the light is too precious. But the really significant change is that we have become transhumant, like the Kazakh herders who shift their homes and herds in response to the changing season. We spend the winter sleeping in a shed tucked in the woods, but come springtime we migrate down to a little caravan on the shore. For a few months we spend much of our days there, cooking as well as sleeping. However, by mid-summer the midgies make full-time life in a small caravan intolerable, particularly because the heat and fumes of cooking attract them and closing the windows creates a sweaty and steamy atmosphere that is unpleasant to sleep in. So, for the summer months we shift our kitchen activities to a cool little old caravan up at the top of the croft, and keep the shore-side caravan fug-and-bug-free for sleeping. Once the insect menace declines in autumn and the evenings start drawing in, we revert to the spring pattern at the loch, until the days get too short, the paths too icy and winter storms too fierce and we retreat to the shelter of the woods and the cycle begins again. A friend joked that she imagined the hushed tones of David Attenborough making a documentary about our strange animal-like behaviour. 'Each year, shortly after the first primroses bloom, the two humans can be seen making their way down to the water's edge ...'

I cannot recommend transhumance highly enough. There is a deep satisfaction that comes from modifying basic sleeping and eating behaviour to suit the season. It is a joy to head out to the light of ripples on water in spring. It is a joy to stroll half a kilometre to bed on a summer's evening. It is a joy to smell autumn woodland smells mingling with sea scents. It is a joy to snuggle up in the snowy woods in winter. The seasonal changes are an acknowledgement of one of the most basic rhythms of life. This is the single biggest improvement that wilding myself has made to my sense of wellbeing.

I want to advocate this to everyone. I know it is difficult for people living in street-lit 24/7 urban environments, I know our societal norm is to work regular 9-to-5 hours regardless of the time of year, and I know this mitigates against any seasonal variations in behaviour; but still, I feel sure everyone can find some way, even just moving the furniture, to respond to the Earth's rotation around the life-giving sun.

❦ ❦ ❦

Behind the sheds, continuing north, a steep slope is swathed in mature mixed woodland of aspen, birch, hazel, willow, oak and rowan. Chaffinches and blue tits make tentative sounds in the watery light. Above a crag, where an ivy rides high on an overhanging aspen, a blackbird pipes. It nests there each spring.

Above, on a flat boggy clearing, is the scar of our recent mistaken attempt to dig a foundation for a cabin, on rock that turned out to be too soft. The resulting hole has filled with water. The disturbed ground around it will heal eventually. I'm pleased by the unexpected boon of a pool, and notice a pond-skater making tiny waves. It will be interesting to watch the succession of life that will inevitably claim it as home.

Over the road that cuts through the top of the croft, the path plunges straight into hazel thicket, steeply uphill again. A great tit calls *cher-tea-cher-tea-cher-tea-cher-tea* from an oak tree. A wren *tut-tut-tuts* from its scolding post. A red deer hind stands on the horizon, ears cocked in a questioning Y. She tips her head out to the west and sniffs, then stares at me, not moving as I approach. Her ears tilt and swivel. Then a car passes on the road below and with a short bark to her hidden companions and followers, she is over the brow of the hill in one bound.

High up at the top of the croft, the old lichen-pocked boundary dyke marks the edge of the common grazings. The gneiss-and-heather landscape rolls away towards the mountains, each standing proud and individual along the horizon, the tips of their summits in cloud, their features etched by snow. I heave deep breaths, my chest rising and falling as I scan their shapes: Canisp, Suilven, Cul Mor, Cul Beg, the four mountains now owned by this land-reform transformed community, then Stac Pollaidh and Ben Mor Coigach further south, and the blur of the Torridon mountains.

My walk began with crows and ends with two ravens soaring over, finger wings carving the sky. I stretch out my arms and wave back to them. I am rewarded with a caw.

a raven swings and rolls
crooning *craw-croo*
soaring between layers
of light and flow

all we need to know
the old man says
is how to be *rahayu*
grateful for this moment

for silver clouds in the relentless sky
and this black wheeling curve of bird

One final paradox: as I have become wilder, the distance between myself and nature seems to have reduced and the croft has come to feel less wild. As the croft gets wilder, I feel increasingly at home. Scrambling the once treacherous path down a crag is now second nature; the inaccessible cove, reached only by abseiling down the cliff, is now a regular haunt; the seemingly random tumble of boulders is a recognisable archaeological relic; I am on first-name terms with once unusual plants and they flower at predictable times (and some, I have to admit, I even pull up as weeds from my vegetable patch). The strange, and possibly dangerous, has become familiar. The wild-out-there has become normal-in-here.

What persists is the sense of sheer wonder at the endless stream of curiosities, beauties and inexplicables that nature creates. The big white mystery of 'the wild' has refracted into a spectrum of intimate multi-coloured little mysteries – 'the wilds'. And maybe I am becoming one of them. I hope so.

The Light and the Line

Jane Alexander

So much depends on the light. When the lid of cloud presses low, when the light is serviceable and thin, I can walk for miles, and nothing lifts.

On the south-eastern edge of the city, I follow the path that tacks up Blackford Hill. The grass is coloured like straw, falls away soft and flat. I am disappointed by the way the landscape is presenting itself to me. Mushy; blurred: there are no bones.

I make my mind into a frame; see in terms of fore, middle and background. I am looking hard, watching for changing angles as the distance reveals itself, step by climbing step. But it's pretence. I can say I'm remaining open, but the landscape holds the cards. When I reach the place that could be a painting, it will show itself, the just-so of all its elements, whether or not I'm searching.

I've come prepared to capture a picture, if I should find one. My sketchpad and pastels stay packed in my rucksack – the one I bought years ago because it's just the right size for airline hand baggage and, stuffed full, will do for as long as any journey takes. I barely use it for travelling, now: now I work less, write more; fly less, walk more; earn less, dream more. Also because take-off and landing feel to me like extraordinary risk – ever since bravado and a shrill desire to live more fully compelled me to drop from a plane, fifty miles north-west of here and 3500 feet above land the patched green and brown of camouflage. The parachute pulled itself, or rather was pulled by a nylon line connecting me, umbilical, to the body of the plane. I hung in a cradle of wind and ripstop, an impossible swing of disbelief: below, the earth was gauzy and unreal.

At the summit of Blackford Hill the wind threatens to knock

me off my feet, roll me back on myself. *And Jill comes tumbling after.*

A week later: pack on my back, I'm walking the old Granton, Leith and Barnton Railway. The rail line is now a bike path: unlike the tracks that circle clockwise from Blackford Hill and still carry freight, this sheltered, wooded route is peopled with runners, cyclists, mothers with buggies. By Roseburn, heading north and east above the Water of Leith, the embankments are tumbled with wild growth. I reach out as I walk: catkins demand to be stroked, leave specks of pollen in the crease-lines of my hand. These fat fuzzy caterpillars were make-believe pets for me each spring: motionless, of course, and still more fun than goldfish.

Early blossom hangs over my head. White petals, pink sepals, a foam-bath froth with the promise of matching fragrance. But when I tug a whippy branch down close to my face, it smells blank. Hawthorn. The May tree, and it's only March: too cold, too early for perfume. The petals are sugar for the eyes, an innocent, fluttering dance.

A few steps further on, flowering currant hangs out rags of flowers like flags for spring. *Ribes:* rich raspberry, the colour for a brunette. In my middle teens I began to learn the shades that suited me. The flowers are dusty pink but deeper; bite-your-lips darker. There's a currant like this that grows in the neighbour's garden, by my bedroom window, and as the year heats up it sends a cattish stink into the room. At night, outside the open window, mating cats yowl.

I move on, past a wave of wild garlic that bears down the embankment. Before the wind it bows in heaps, wet and fat green: a cool bed of leaves, with a sharp crushed smell. In front, a stem of cow parsley stands alone, mouseback-grey skeleton of last summer. Spent flower-heads are upturned umbrellas, each spoke topped by another tiny umbrella, sticking it out through winter.

At snail's pace I progress, bending, peering, stretching; noting shapes and colours. On pages made from trees – pulped, boiled, laid – I trace trunks and branches, using charcoal blackened from willow twigs; graphite and clay dug from the earth and hugged in a casing of incense cedar; pastels, their pigment bound with sap from acacia trees, or shiraz gum from milkvetch root. With what's been taken from her, I play at re-creating nature. And for all her richness, what she's offering is detail, and surface. The bones are missing still.

The third week: I'm down by the Cramond shoreline, the end of the cycle route that runs from Roseburn. It's a day of racing weather. The wind chops the sea into brilliants. The sky is washed in two halves, Ultramarine and Paynes Gray, and saturated with magical, muscular light. My rucksack squats open-mouthed at my feet; I pull out my sketchbook. With a blunt graphite stump I place two lines on the page.

Where land curves into the sea – in the congruence of three kinds of space – right here is the picture.

Air is a dream-space, clear, streaked, thin. That skydive tingles in my palms and the soles of my feet. I remember reading somewhere that people look up when they think of the future. Probably, it was the same magazine that ran a piece on the way you eat an apple, and how it can display your personality. (Turn it backwards as you bite and you reveal a tendency to focus on the past; forwards, and…) But I've caught myself building castles in the air, staring skywards. Perhaps the apple psychology is true, too.

When you think of the past, your gaze falls to earth, to the second kind of space. This is where you feel the blunt reassurance of your soles on certain ground. This is what can't be changed; what's concrete, as in actual, but the antithesis of actual concrete – earth in your fingers, dirty hands, and underfoot the slip of sand, the spring of marram grass.

The third, gleaming space wasn't mentioned in the magazine. In it, you see yourself: lose yourself. It bears your weight. It pulls you under. It conceals unknown depths. It's transparent, and opaque, the opposite of itself. At the shore, I trail my fingers through the water's cold shock, see them lengthened, curled, like pink clean prawns. Further out, silt thins the light; depth creates darkness.

And when I paint, it's both dark and light, and I know I could try my whole life and never get it right. It shows itself only to the edge of my gaze: I stare at it slantways, the way you stare at a waiting grave.

Air, earth, water: they bump up against each other, and they form the line. Except, there is no such thing as a line. The art teacher tells us so, in primary school probably, secondary certainly. But the line is there when I look for it, as actual as the Earth. Rough, fat or hair-thin, it can scrape and spike and scribble, can swoop and curve, can falter or be bold, or blurred, can make a statement, ask a question, be stabbing, strict or gentle, tight or loose. It's all of these things, and it leads me: it's something to cling to, like sense, like story. It's a summary, as in line drawing; a symbol for something familiar. It's the shape of the whole horizon, as much of the world as any one of us can see.

Staring at my perfect curve, I look in three ways at once – or perhaps I'm switching ways of looking, so fast they seem to overlap. I look at what's in front of me, see it as itself. I look in the same way at the marks I'm making on the page. And I look at what doesn't yet exist: at how I'll create this later, in paint. With half-closed eyes I measure tones against each other. I learn that the bright half of the sky, unexpectedly, is darker than the sea. Layering pastels, I finger-mix the soft dust on the page, trying to catch the colours. I blur the line of the horizon, which is the same as using ten words where five will do – except that those spare words can be edited out. My charcoal line can't be unblurred. I take a fresh page.

Week four: working in the studio. The destination, now, is the finished painting.

I tape my sketches to the wall, each a single version of what I saw. The sketches are notes, reminders only: what counts is to conjure back that high, wide space. With paint on board, I try to recreate the spot where I stood and said a quiet yes. It's the space that allows me to lengthen the line, to darken the sky. As any writer knows, you can make things up that will tell the truth.

With painting, I know sooner than with writing whether it will fail; more often than not, it does. But it's easier too, to point at where it's gone wrong; to learn, and try again.

Either way – success or failure – it's the witnessing that counts. Because in the end, isn't it just to say: I was here? With the Earth below me, the sky above, staring aslant at the mystery of water. I lived through this moment, this green consolation; I lived, just as the hawthorn lived, the willow, the marram grass. Sun and wind, I felt the world against my skin.

By the shore I heard a herring-gull call that it, too, was living.

The wind punched into the sea, and a rainbow vanished as soon as it appeared.

This is what I saw. It made me feel.

This is what I felt.

Sewing a Seam on the Spirit Line

Lisa Samson

I'll drink the emptiness of rain, sky, rock
lie in ferns and harts-tongue
with my own tongue stilled, bridled
for ravens' cries to mock.

Mort, G. *Sky Burial* (1989)

I am blown down the farm track to the shiny slate roofs of Muker, chased by a glowering cloud mass that swept away the blue sky above the moors only minutes earlier. Cold blasts of air numb my cheeks and fingertips and nibble at my nose; a shock after the midday warmth. Pinpricks of hail make pock marks on the velvet moorland but under the snug of my hood I hear only my own heart pumping rapidly in time with my ragged breath. I have been walking now for hours and, as the accustomed movement takes over, I become a mere physical being, no thoughts in my head, just the beat of my feet over turf and stone. This physicality, this discovery of the self without words, for me can occur only during sex or hiking, when my body builds up its own momentum, my heart beats to its own tune, and I act on instinct, becoming more animal than human. Mindlessly, I descend the moors as dusk draws early over the dale and the wood fires smouldering on the cold air welcome me to Muker.

I have just climbed down Kisdon Hill, that swells high above the road between Keld and Muker, a hard glacial deposit that even the downy turf on its flanks cannot soften. When I clambered up the steep bridleway from Keld, I thought that the pallbearers in mediaeval times chose the most difficult route possible to Muker. For this is the first part of the old Corpse Way, where the mediaeval village dwellers of Keld and Tan Hill used to carry their dead to the consecrated ground in the churchyard, fourteen miles away in Grinton. In mediaeval times they believed that the soul would be damned for eternity if the body was not buried in hallowed ground. It used to take the pallbearers a full two or three days to descend from their lonely upper dale along the banks of the Swale, depending on how much they drank at the pubs en route. When they undertook their sombre task they often had to contend with harsh conditions and they would not have been as well-equipped as me, with my warm waterproofs and hardy boots. Yet my feet are only gently skimming the surface of the Corpse Way, like dressmaker's chalk sketching a soft line round the valley, tracing the indelible footprints of generations of pallbearers who trudged these fells over four centuries, until Muker was granted its own consecrated ground in 1580.

The first part of the way up Kisdon Hill is rough, with stones loose underfoot until the track curves round near a farm and evens out into a steady slope up to an area called Shake Holes. The route goes along the ridge of the steep hillside, because the Swale, with its historic reputation as the fastest rising river in Britain, could be treacherous in winter floods, and there are tales of pallbearers being swept away. From the top of Shake Holes you can see for miles on either side: the stone farm buildings camouflaged brown in their shadowy nook surrounded by uneven strips of fields, and the snow-streaked fells on the tops. If you look northwards to the end of the valley, the grey sky seems to go on and on before it ends in a curved line, like a headland approaching the sea. I watched the curlews arching and dipping over the moor, their high-pitched call spiralling into a feverish lament, each note curling into the next, getting faster and faster.

In recent weeks my feet have been trudging in a back-stitch pattern back and forth over the river Swale and parts of the Corpse Way, beginning at various villages along the way then looping back on myself: today from Muker to Tan Hill and back again, last week from Muker to Gunnerside. There is never quite enough time to walk the full fourteen-mile stretch from Keld to Grinton in a day-trip from my home. I stumbled across the Corpse Way only recently and, fuelled partly by a fascination with the people's blind faith in the tenets of their religion, and partly by my family's association with the area, it has become a kind of personal pilgrimage. Since I follow no particular faith and believe only in the healing powers of the earth, the natural cycle of the seasons and our own evolution, this landscape is my cathedral. In some weathers, it is harsh and unforgiving, and I come up here to be battered about by the elements, for as an agnostic I have no confessional, no means of atoning for sins, and my strength to forgive is gathered here.

There are many Corpse Ways or lych ways up and down Britain but most of them have fallen into disuse, though traditionally these routes to the churchyards became public rights of way. In mediaeval times they believed that the spirits needed a free passage up and down these spirit lines, and for this reason the land it traversed had to be unploughed, clear of gates and hedgerows. The Swaledale Corpse Way is one of the longest and is still well used; locals walk en masse along it on Good Fridays, a kind of ancestral pilgrimage.

I stand a moment as the wind blows my hood back and whips my hair round my face, and look down the gritty ridge where rough boulders balance precariously on the steep sides of the valley. I breathe in the air as fresh as the seaside, the raw gusts of wind that sting my eyes and make my ears ache; a communion of wind and ice that leaves me cleansed. The wind rising through the branches of the trees gathers force, reminds me of waves crashing on rocks, but there is another sound as well, of clinking metal, and I recall that once this valley rang with the hammers of lead miners. In my mind's eye I see a flickering line of lights moving as one along the valley, the lead miners returning home to Muker after a hard day underground, the valley echoing with their footsteps and gruff voices. Sometimes it was so cold that their clothes froze as they walked and icicles were hanging from them when they arrived home.

Yet we are nowhere near the sea; we are in the middle of England, round the upper lumbar region of England's backbone, in the dale of Swale where the locals show their attachment to their land by choosing one of their own gateposts for a headstone before they die. And though scars have been left by the lead mines and slate quarries, they have long fallen into disuse. The old quarry above Keld looks as if Wade (the giant who legend has it formed Northumbria by throwing a huge boulder) has bitten into it with his giant gnashers, leaving the open wound to fester. Even years of careful environmental planning, reconstruction and planting, would not be able to heal this scar. But I am from the mining area of Doncaster, where abandoned open cast pits are part of the landscape, nestling amongst their own slag heaps. In comparison, I am humbled by the grand scale of the world up here, by this landscape whose geology has remained relatively intact since mediaeval times.

The light in the valley is as variable as the colours of the sea: the ever-changing hues of grey-blue rock, brown earth, red bracken and greens of grass and tree can only be caught by the living eye or moving images. It has become the wild landscape of my imagination, and if I were an artist, as my parents both are, I would be able to paint it from memory. In those still hours of my childhood, sitting beside my parents or standing behind them as they painted, I absorbed their perspective of the natural world and their intense concentration. Yet no amount of imaginary painting captures what I want to express about this landscape: the raw wind whipping trees and bracken high on the moors, the cast of the shadows and the coconut scent of yellow gorse in spring.

It is early March, the first warm spring-like day of the year; and when I set out this morning the peat bounced beneath my feet and my heart was full. A day out alone on these fells with my dog felt like a gift, and I was reminded of the last stanza of Edward Thomas' poem *March the Third:*

This day unpromised is more dear
Than all the days of the year
When seasonable sweets come in
Because we know how lucky we are

A wood pigeon cooed at my back and the dew formed a thin film of mist above the meadow, where the sweet sap rose from the grasses I crushed under my feet. 'Keep to the path', the sign warned, for these are the natural meadows of Muker, cut in the traditional method of the Dales and tended in the same way since mediaeval times. No fertilisers are used and the fields are allowed to grow hay, unlike modern methods in which the grass is cut three times a year. In May these meadows will be dancing with the pretty heads of buttercups, cow parsley, pink clover and mountain pansies. Whenever I come here I am touched by the tenderness of the locals who care for the land in this way.

Save for a single figure on the ridge of the valley below Shake Holes Scar, I was the only human about, since my companion was my dog, transformed to feral predator in this pastureland where he could smell sheep a mile distant. Ears pricked, nose to the ground, features sharpened like a wolf, he strained at the leash, nearly dragging me down the narrow stone steps to the river.

The cattle that sometimes block our route were not there, and I wondered whether they were gone to be milked or slaughtered.

I turned left to follow the Swale to Keld along the dark side of the valley, walking upstream the way the pallbearers might have returned home. Ahead of me, a fir wood was tumbling down the lowest slopes to the water as if the pointed treetops were in a race to nosedive into the river to drink. They contrasted with the softer, fuller shapes of the ash, beech and hawthorn that are indigenous to this landscape. My grandfather, a native of the South Riding of Yorkshire, told me that the Romans carried the saplings of fir trees from Italy to northern England all those centuries ago. Most people assume that it is a natural feature of the landscape, but they and the wild flower meadows must be the only designed adornment in this otherwise raw and exploited valley. A little further on across the river are the ruins of the smelting plant at Swinner Gill.

The burnished reds and browns of winter have turned to dappled greens dancing in the sunshine. On the other side of the river I could see Swaledale sheep climbing the scattered boulders, weaving in between birches that lean at thirty-degree angles from their craggy outcrops. Swaledale sheep are known for their home-loving qualities; they never stray far from their own grazing grounds. Above me, on a ridge carved into the hillside like string tight round a side of beef, a young farm worker loaded his quad bike truck with hazel logs, leaving a trail of fresh sawdust in his wake, the dry innards of young deadwood. He stared at me curiously, at the lone female intruding on his working solitude with my big black dog. Despite my unkempt appearance, I knew that the curl of my hair was city cut and my boots smart suede.

I passed a tumbledown cottage, and a disturbed grouse beat a hefty retreat out of the hole where the roof should be, its throttled cry like the starter motor of a 50-cc scooter, heralding its distress. Pausing a moment, I peered through a window space and saw a rough-hewn stone staircase, curving up to a few rotten beams, all that remained of the first floor. Doorless cupboards gaped in the corner of the old kitchen, its only inhabitants spiders, field mice and the odd grouse.

All over these hills are dotted disused dwellings of stone and slate, some shepherds' huts, some lead miners' cottages, abandoned since the early nineteen-hundreds, when the lead seams had been exhausted and many of the miners migrated to the industrial cities and towns. This and neighbouring valleys were mined intensively for lead during the 17th and 19th centuries, though it had been established as the main form of industry in the dale before mediaeval times. There is evidence that dates lead mining in the area back to the Romans. There were some quarries but sheep farming and knitting were the other main forms of livelihood. In the 18th and 19th centuries, men, women and children all took part in the carding, spinning and knitting. For the lead miners, daylight hours were scarce, so they perfected a method of knitting stockings as they walked to and from the mines. Extraordinary though this seems, they wore a knitting sheath round their waist and used curved needles that enabled them to knit with short circular movements of the hands, building up a rhythm to walk by.

I sat on a slimy rock to eat cake that crumbled into the crevices where turf and stone have moulded together. Below me, a lapwing squeaked as it circled the sparkling water and settled on a flat stone, its long orange beak dipping close to the water where a sheep was drinking. In the 19th century this river would have been a rich tea-brown from the lead smelting plant upstream. Behind it, the double hump of Arn Gill rises steeply, split in two by a trickle of stream that comes down between them; this I imagine to be the backside of the giant Wade. My dog wrenched at his lead and plunged downhill to the sheep. A flimsy chicken-wire fence halted him momentarily, buying me just enough time to grasp the lead and drag my domestic wolf back to the track.

I was now climbing the muddy path into Kisdon Wood, where the dank green tongue of lichen has licked stone and branch alike, furring the arteries of the woodland's heart, where ivy has wrapped its insinuating fingers thrice round the tree trunks, choking the life sap out of the sinewy grey limbs of an old birch tree, now brittle and wrinkled as an elephant's hide. Under this dark canopy of leaves we followed the steep path where only a crumbling dry stone wall shielded us from the sheer death drop to Kisdon Force below, passing an old lime kiln tucked away in a mound to our right.

My dog chose this moment to make his escape. Wrenching free of the leash, he launched down the side of the ravine, causing startled sheep to bleat a hasty retreat. I called his name, in vain, my voice echoed round the valley, bounced back to me as I gazed, impotent, down the steep drop, the frightened flock milling around me. He ignored my pleas and, abandoned, I began to feel uneasy, alone in that dense eerie wood. Nearby was a curly hawthorn, its twisted branches like my fuzzy hair blown by the wind. I took refuge by curving my body into its side, resting my head on its gnarled trunk, kindred spirits in this wilderness. After an hour or so the dog returned, mouth frothing, dark flanks sleek with sweat. He was lucky not to have been shot by the farmer.

I set off once again down that stony path, beaten by centuries of passing footsteps, which for me has become a walk in the valley of the shadow of death, though it is far below the Corpse Way. For it leads me to the burnt bones of my beautiful sister, whose ashes are buried underneath her rowan tree at East Gill Force. Its spring blossoms are her beauty now, and its red berries, that in summer glow against the metallic grey of the cliff, are her blood. Jane was thirty when she died, a good age for a mediaeval woman, but pitiful by today's standards. The spindly arms of her tree reach skyward, sheltered from the weather by the shallow bracelet of limestone that encloses East Gill Force. I'm glad that she is near the silvery spray of the waterfall, where my dad dipped my infant, Daniel, into its foaming waters fifteen years ago, an incidental baptism; the only one he's ever had. The waters of the Swale were once believed to be sanctified and it was known as 'the holy river'. Between 627 and 633 AD, St Paulinus, monk and first bishop of York, is said to have baptised ten thousand people in this river, following the decision of the pagan high priest, Coifi, to abandon the service of the pagan gods.

It was on that shimmering summer day in 1994 that my family discovered this valley for the first time, when on a holiday to Reeth my sister and her boyfriend led us down to the Swale. Jane had to pull me the last stretch through the cow meadow to Muker; I was still slow and lumbering after childbirth, nothing like my easy stride of today. That was the last time that we walked all together as a family, when Jane was still alive. If I'd known then it was the last time I'd walk with her, I'd have clung to her hand, lingered by the water's edge until dusk and whispered our sibling secrets in the sweet meadow haze of that balmy night. Since then I have returned so many times that I believe I could find my way easily in the dark.

She is safe here, with Kisdon Woods rising darkly to the west and Beldi Hill above her, three feet under this soft ground below the village of Keld (Keld means 'running water' in Norse). Proud silver birches, sentinels to guard this lush watering hole, flank curly hawthorns that bend to drink at the water. The hawthorn is supposed to be a symbol of hope and is said to be able to heal a broken heart. Behind Jane's tree, the corpses of two beeches rest: one on its side, humbly prostrate for walkers to rest on, its bark stripped by ravenous cows, the other sadly gesturing skywards, its desecrated body gnawed at by badgers, wind and rain.

Jane is the guardian angel of these crossroads, for this is where the Pennine Way crosses the coast to coast footpath, and in Celtic mythology crossroads are said to be where the underworld meets the celestial, potentially dangerous places that need the protection of a saint or guardian angel. Rowan trees are said to offer protection against witches. This is unconsecrated ground that our mediaeval forebears would have been horrified to be buried in, but for us it seemed a sacred resting hole. We are not the only ones to choose the Swale as a resting place for our loved ones; Graham Mort, the poet, also scattered his parents' ashes in the River Swale, because it is the location of family memories precious to them. Here are the first three stanzas of *Apis Aphasia,* the poem he wrote about this valley:

Muker is Norse: Keld, Gunnerside, Thwaite, all
migrant-named, the tongue rolling in foreign grit;
noon heat climbs as stratus in sky's china-blue,
spreading a mycelium spawn. Turned headstones
pave meadows, face-down on their holy texts, their dates
invisibly opening and closing; these field gates sprung
with steel coil – where an old boot sole served once –
snap us against stone uprights.

That ether of honey is clover, bistort, cranesbill,
buttercup, the pale frocks of fool's parsley; not one
bee thrumming in foxgloves or stumbling in crammed
cargo pants of pollen or propolis. Their colonies fail –
even pheromones fade there – the body language
for each flower lost at the hive's entry where sentries
have found sleep, its finger-tight hole the well-
spring of our everlasting dark.

> *The Swale is quick here; once I scrambled out, let*
> *my parents slip away: grey dust, brown water, a long*
> *soft syllable of ash, curlews liquifying sex above.*
> *The gable of the farm where I dreamed some other*
> *life has burst to a buttress of spilled stone, dis-*
> *tempered walls, a century's laminate of filth; we watch*
> *a dipper feeding one fat chick, its screams teetering*
> *on the cusp of hunger and self-love.*

Another weekend, in early April now, and my friend Lizzie Bear and I have arrived to walk the full fourteen miles of the Corpse Way. Lizzie is a better map reader than me, and I'm hoping she will unravel the ancient byway from the maze of footpaths that cross this valley, once walked daily by the lead miners to and from the mines and smelting mills. Tracing the spirit line on the map with my finger in the pub the night before was as easy as tacking a rough seam to sew over. But I know myself, my sewing was always as haphazard as my map reading, and I need Lizzie to unknot the thread that will lead us along the sections of the Corpse Way I have not yet walked.

The morning we set out from Keld, we are pelted by sheets of icy rain as we climb Kisdon Hill. Over the last week the cold winds have returned to the North, blowing the heads off dancing daffodils, sweeping fresh blossom in its wake, wiping away the warmth of that mild early March. Yet the sweet scents of spring linger on the damp morning air, and as we cross the bridge below Muker and turn right for Ivelet and Gunnerside, the sun gleams between the clouds. This is one of the crossing places of the Corpse Way, where the pallbearers would lift the corpse bodily across running water using stepping stones or a bridge. The dead were carried with their feet directed away from home, toward the burial ground. This was believed to be a method of preventing the dead from trying to return home in spirit form to haunt the living, since superstition held that spirits could not cross water.

Here, the land plateaus out and the vegetation is lusher, tamer than the upper valley. It is gentle and undulating, and would have come as light relief to the pallbearers carrying their dead in a wicker basket. This is pretty pastureland, relatively flat, easy walking after the grinding stony climb up Kisdon Hill. Just below Ivelet Bridge a strip of the shore has crumbled and separated from the mainland to form a shallow ravine, evidence that erosion is taking place. Near here a hillock swells above the Swale, but the downy grass cannot hide the strips carved into its side, once agricultural steps created in the same way as vine terraces in Tuscany. These are 'lynchets' ploughed by Anglo-Saxons with oxen and planted with wheat, barley and oats.

On Ivelet Bridge is an ancient corpse stone where the pallbearers used to rest their burden. Now it leans precariously towards the river, and any corpse laid there would undoubtedly slip into the water and get washed downstream. There are tales of a headless dog that is said to bring bad luck to all who see it on the bridge at Ivelet. When I investigate I discover that there are many such tales of dogs linked to spirit ways, that have both negative and positive connotations. Big black dogs in particular (like my own) figure prominently and there was a belief that dogs were the spiritual guardians of these lych roads.

The Corpse Way rises steeply above Gunnerside, where Swaledale sheep graze contentedly on the soft turf, known locally as 'allotment land' because it is the rough common land between the meadows and the moorland. As we follow the track up to the higher slopes, where the burnished bracken resembles scatterings of seaweed on the sea shore, I sit down to adjust my boots and look back down the valley: at the verdant flat fields that meet the river in higgledy-piggledy strips. These small land enclosures, or 'intacks', are the water meadows irrigated by the Norsemen who operated a rota system of allotting land on an annual basis, so that each smallholder had their chance to benefit from the superior crop yield of the fertile land. In the trees above we hear the glottal cough of the grouse echoing fearfully and the sheep call to one another across the valley.

By an odd twist of fate, the boots I am wearing are my mother's; we accidentally swapped when she left hers in my garage and I left mine in her car. Since starting out this morning, I have found myself looking at things as she would, staring for ages at the angle of the trees in their craggy outcrop, as if measuring the perspective for a sketch. Now I compare the squares and oblongs of fields, with their rich red hues, graduating to lime patches, to a patchwork quilt she once made. She is a skilled seamstress and designer, as was her mother before her. 'You must get the tonal arrangement right,' I hear her say, meaning the contrast of darkness with light, the shadows and sunny patches of the scene below. Here, nature has made its own tonal arrangement and the result is a beautiful silken cloth spread over the long valley to the white-streaked tops above Keld, where smoke from heather fires billows on the high moors.

The path climbs steeply above us to a rocky ridge that marks a higher footpath following the tyre swerves of the farmer's quad bike, up to the ruins of the lead mines at Gunnersgill on the moors above, where shafts bore deep into the hillside. Here, a row of hawthorn trees has bent inwards to the hillside for protection from the harsh winds. One of them has had its bark stripped by sheep or cows, exposing bleached wood shaped like a human femur bone.

The river wending its way down the valley curves with the generous sweep of a hemline on a full skirt. We press on to the high ridge that will lead us to the Dead House at Blades where the pallbearers used to leave the corpse to rest overnight, while they drank and slept at the Punch Bowl in Low Row. On top of the ridge the sun comes out and casts squat shadows of our figures, giving us distorted body shapes that make us look like trolls crawling along the brow of the hill. For the pallbearers it would be the close of a weary day's march and they would be looking forward to their refreshment at The Punch Bowl Inn. I imagine the commotion their arrival would make in the village at Blades, what a striking scene the pallbearers would have made holding their sacred burden aloft in its wicker basket, a gaggle of barefoot, knotty-haired children trailing behind them and peering into the Dead House.

At lonely, windswept Blades, above Feetham (from Fitjum, Norse for meadow), we linger to search for the ruin of the Dead House, but of the two crumbling remains of buildings in the village, both look equally desolate and worthy of the name 'dead house'. So we practically run down the easy track to Low Row, calling excitedly to each other over the wind about what we will eat and drink when we get there. Sheep wander across the green, in between the numerous cars parked along the road below the Punch Bowl Inn.

'The food must be great!' cries Lizzie.

A couple, dressed smartly in black, walk purposefully up to the inn in front of us and, as we approach, we realise there is a funeral going on inside. A sign on the door reads 'Closed due to unforeseen circumstances'. We groan and hold our aching bellies in dismay. We've brought no food with us and were relying on this for our halfway sustenance, like the pallbearers before us. We sit on the bench outside the church and break a tight satsuma into segments that we suck sorely, bitter sweet.

Checking the map, we choose the path that rises to the left above the road out of Low Row, and drag our weary feet uphill. Hunger gnawing at my belly and the sun now beating down on me, I begin to feel light-headed. When I was little, my grandmother, my mother's mother, used to give me a fat blunt needle to sew the pieces of her knitting together into a baby's jacket or a doll's cardigan. Although I went through all the right motions, licking the wool to make it easier to thread and then sewing as tightly as possible, it used to take me an afternoon to make any progress, dropping as many stitches as I sewed. I experience again that intense frustration, placing my feet one in front of the other over the rough woolly grasses, yet never seeming to get any further.

Finally, at the top of the hill, we argue over which direction is the Corpse Way. Since there are no signs to guide us, I decide we should let our feet instinctively find the right track, that will surely be compressed by centuries of footfall. Lizzie is having none of it, and insists that we follow the obvious route, above the houses. At this point I'm sure we are going off course but all I want is to find some food. In mediaeval times the pallbearers would sometimes carry the corpse straight through houses or go close to them, because the spirit line had to be as straight as possible. Since we don't know where the houses would have been in those days, it is hard to know if we are off course, but I know the seam we are sewing is jagged.

We climb up as if we are heading for Reeth Moor, where the grasses are bleached by sun and wind and Calver Hill protrudes like a moon crater. Up there, small humps or deposits from the Old Gang smelting mines add to the effect of a pock-marked moonscape. Wind-burnt and bone-weary, we turn away from the moors and as we go right towards Healaugh, at the top of a farm track, we are startled by nine stark white doves that circle over the road in front of us and flit up to the high ground. It seems fortuitous that they chose to cross our path at that precise moment; a portent of good times rolling ahead. It is the time of evening when the shadows are at their longest and the sun, low in the sky, sheds its last pink glow over the fells, wreathing the heather in its golden kiss, promising us a long evening and another bright day ahead.

At Healaugh we wander fruitlessly round the village looking for the post office marked on the map, in the vain hope that we might buy some chocolate to keep us going. No such luck, though there is a footpath marked clearly across the fields by the river to Reeth, which we are sure is the route of the Corpse Way. The Manor House sign swings forlornly on the side of an unostentatious building that in mediaeval times was the centre of a large estate extending to forty thousand acres. We fly across the pretty pasture land to Reeth, though once in sight of its kind stone houses tucked into the hillside, our limbs start to ache and we just manage to drag ourselves into the nearest teashop.

Fortunately, the final stretch to Grinton is the easiest of the whole spirit way, and with full bellies we lumber across a flat field where tiny new lambs frolic. Ahead of us, the spire of Grinton Church protrudes above the trees, though in mediaeval times it was one long, single-storey building, and the view the pallbearers would have as they approached from the West would have been of the round headed Norman window, now enclosed by an extension. The pallbearers' hearts must have lifted at the sight of that window as they dragged their aching limbs to the 'Cathedral of the Dale', so-called because it served the whole parish from where Swaledale borders Cumbria in the West, to Marrick, two miles east of here.

The churchyard that awaits us is still and overgrown, warmed by the early evening sunshine, where the crumbling coffin stones of local farmers and 18th-century lead miners vie for space with the cleaner headstones of their 20th-century descendants. The bones and skulls of their mediaeval forebears must be buried under another seam of earth and rubble, compressed by the weight of five centuries' corpses. I am glad that my sister is not in this overcrowded consecrated ground, but rests in the fertile earth below Keld, with the waterfall to herself.

In this cruel century, on this overcrowded island, all wild places are now sacred land. The pallbearers carried their dead fourteen miles to bury them in consecrated ground, trudging over land which city dwellers now travel miles to hike through on Sundays. If 'to consecrate' means 'to sanctify', then by the urbanisation of our country we have unwittingly sanctified that land which is still free. In this dale, we have dug into the rich seams that yield lead ore, cut into the earth's veins for metals, leaving sutures that even the years' passing cannot heal, scars staunched but still visible on the fell sides. These open wounds have been reclaimed by nature, become part of the wilderness once again, symbolic of the natives' dependency on their land and of the symbiosis between people and the earth.

That night I lie awake, listening to the beck gushing through Muker, just below our window. It soothes my aching mind, and when I sleep I dream of sliding down scree slopes, slipping further and further into a dark tunnel like a mine shaft under the moors. My body rouses itself before I hit the bottom, and I know that my survival instinct is intact; it will be a long time before I slide underground.

For now, I've sewn my jagged seam along the spirit line, and confirmed what I already know, that the wild upper valley is my heart's home. This valley is where my sons will scatter me, when my time comes, that our sibling souls might splash in the springs of the Swale, dance over cow parsley and cicely, together again, me and Jane. We will 'drink the emptiness of rain, sky, rock'[1] and lie in a tight embrace in the shelter of the rowan tree.

Bibliography

Cooper, E (1962) *Muker: the Story of a Yorkshire Parish* Dalesman Publishing Company: Clapham, Yorkshire

---

[1] Mort, 1989, p57.

Hartley, M. Ingilby, J (1969) *The Old Hand Knitters of the Dales* Dalesman Publishing Company: Clapham, Yorkshire

Morris, D (1994) *The Swale: A History of the Holy River of St Paulinus* The Ebor Press: York

Mort, G *Sky Burial* (1989) Dangaroo Press: Australia

Pennick, N (1996) *Celtic Sacred Landscapes.* Thames & Hudson: London

Thomas, E. (1964) *Selected Poems of Edward Thomas* Faber and Faber: London

Wilkinson, G (1973) *Trees in the Wild* Stephen Hope Books Ltd: London

The Hill

Alison Grant

It takes twenty five minutes to walk up from the Lower Haugh to the hill land. I stride up the Steenie Brae, past the Nine Acre and the South Pound, through the ribbon of leggy pine and up into the space and sudden blast which is the Hill.

Behind me, trees heave against the wind. Collapsed trunks lean and bolster. Branches rub, the flat creaks sawing in the breeze. Four yellow-eyed ewes back up against the dyke. Black crows jostle and carp.

Ahead lies an even slope, rising to a slightly domed skyline, reaching east and west as far as I can see. In summer the heat quivers in the distance, insects thrum and the sky is so high that the larksong seems to spill from nothingness.

But this is February. Pressed grass, stained brown-black, prints a depression where snow lay barely a week ago. Springs leak into a myriad of tiny glinting pools which sit above the sodden earth. Rushes are bleached soft orange. The sky lurks grey and low, clouds curdled with a pale yellow light. There are no buzzing insects.

Half a mile away, pink-footed geese tug at an incongruous patch of green behind a slumped relict fence. They see me coming and shift restlessly, barking calls before rising as one on thudding wing beats. For a fleeting moment, the density of their wings creates a chaotic shimmer, hovering shoal-like just above the ground. Then they surge upwards, swelling along an arc, arranging and re-arranging themselves until a fine dense line forms a leading edge, dragging the speckled flock north across the valley. I listen as the disjointed crackle of their cries softens to mewing with distance.

This land is the edge of things, caught between the remote clefts and fastness of the vast upper moors and the cultivated accessibility of the lower fields. It is a transitional space. A borderland. A mongrel. Neither full-blown moor, nor cultivated field, it adopts characteristics of both. The topography of curving, convex slopes extends down from the uplands while vegetation and human traces nudge upwards from the lowlands.

The result is marginal land. Partially and poorly drained, rushes dominate, mostly. It is grazed lightly, and in summer only. The grass is rough, thin pickings, but dappled and flowery rich. It is limed infrequently – my brother tells me no more than once every ten years, and perhaps not even that – so that heather still sprouts along the march fence, appearing in dark tufts across the drier ridges. The terrain is trackless, with only the occasional rivulet of sheep path, but like a field it has a name – the Hill – although unlike a field it is an open-ended, unspecific title, named, it would seem, as an after thought, with no reflection on its singular nature.

In fact, it is not even hill-shaped. Its highest point is a long ridge, ranging out along an even contour for several miles, flattened against the edge of a high moorland plateau. This plateau in turn reaches back towards further ridges before rising into a line of hills, each with a distinctive, rounded summit. But they seem distant. Between here and there lies heathery moor, torn with peat hags and occasional banks of clumpy grass, and standing pools, called flows, and bogs which sink and slurp against your ankles.

The Hill, then, is marginal land. A ribbon which straddles moor and field, extending like a tideline above the head dyke. It ebbs downwards where north-facing gulleys, thick with whin, trickle between high up fields. It flows upwards where south facing pasture, ploughed and re-sown, tightly drained and crisply edged, climbs onto a steep flank. Such pioneering fields appear to teeter on the edge of cultivation, at all times close to reversion back to boggy breaks and wiry grass.

This landscape shape-shifts. The rough grassland here can easily be subsumed by forestry, or be drained and ploughed when more fodder is required. During the Second World War, extra subsidies were given to Scottish farmers to encourage the home-breeding of cattle on marginal land. Thousands of additional acres went under the plough, in places for the first time in centuries. The land on which I am walking now, a dry hulk of ridge, like the upturned keel of a huge boat, was one such area. Wildness retreated, pushed back into the heart of the moor by a skinny-framed, cab-less tractor tilted into the furrow-bed, crumbling a shallow tilth for 'neeps', orange-fleshed swedes which were used as winter feed for the extra stock.

Nor was it the first time. Look east in the slanted, ripe light of a late summer evening and you can pick out wide curving rigs, carved by mouldboard ploughs pulled by oxen, at any time between three and seven hundred years ago. Imagine that first slice, as that first man – or was it men? – leaned and yelled, adding their weight to the wooden shaft as it caught the earth. Then the first sod, heavy and gleaming, damp-smelling; turning and folding. They lie there still, ridges happed year on year, like pliant ribs bedded snugly, cheek-by-jowl, across broad gentle slopes. They are remnants of a period of warmer summers, when even at this altitude it was possible to produce an oat harvest in reliable succession, one year after the next.

Today, behind these slopes, cast white against a dark blue stain of sky, a long reach of wind turbines stretches across the horizon. In the centre, a guddle of ungainly arms kick and flicker, but at the edges stand single turbines, rhythmically combing energy from the air.

Wind farms are the latest experiment to occupy these unloved edge-lands. Too high, too wet and too rough to support long term viable agriculture in the current climate, but not secluded or untrammelled enough to be valued for their remoteness or naturalness, these places are tugged back and forth between wildness and human endeavour. Cultivation rises then subsides. Stock is increased, grazing the heather out of the hill, then removed as a rump of hillside is planted with spruce trees which sprout into a dense, blue-green encrustation. The trees in their turn are felled to make way for a telecommunication mast or wind turbines. Now there is talk of re-wilding such places, as remaining sheep and cattle are removed and heather and self-seeded clumps of bristling young birch winkle their way between long tufts of ungrazed grass.

But today I am thinking that we may be past re-wilding land like this. On this bit of hill no trees or wind turbines have been planted. Since the war-sown neeps were harvested sixty years ago, the land has been managed with a light touch. Over the intervening decades, wildness has seeped downhill. Close your eyes and sense the unravelling space. Hear the squelch beneath your feet, feel the rough folds of the land. A peewit rises and its call cranks into a plaintive stutter as it lunges upwards. Open your eyes and catch sight of a hare quickening across the skyline. It is already a place that gravitates towards the natural.

Nevertheless, if the climate changes as predicted, this hill land sits in a part of the world where in the future, winters will be wetter and summers drier than for several centuries. As land elsewhere becomes desert and flood, perhaps the Hill will be once more pressed into service. If so, it will be partially drained and cultivation will yet again advance while wildness recedes.

The wind has dropped, and the arms of the turbines have slowed. Flakes of thin snow, light as ash, flick through the air. And the world shrinks. The wind farm disappears completely within seconds. As the snow thickens, the fences dissolve. It is as if I am in an opaque, grey-tinted bubble, half a field in diameter. I drop downhill, my boots slapping lightly on a thin layer of wet snow resting tentatively on lank, tired grass. The high moor disappears and the shelterbelt appears before me as a flat grey band.

I make my way down through the trees and over the dyke to the Mak'm Rich, an ironic name for any field if there ever was one. Only twice in my lifetime have I seen it ploughed, and then the stoney surface, where shining pebbles stood proud of the soil in the rain, was never going to make any farmer rich. But I am back onto fields, each one known as an individual; quirks of soil, drainage, gradient and aspect intimately understood and expressed.

Behind me, now drenched white, is the Hill.

Echoing Lands

Raja Shehadeh

I come from a land of hills full of stories that the lingering ghosts of those who once lived there want to tell. I did not know the same was true of the Scottish Highlands.

I still remember my first encounter with the Highland moors. It was the autumn of 1992. My wife, Penny, and I had booked at the Inveroran Hotel in Glen Orchy near the bridge with the same name. We had chosen this hotel because Wordsworth and his sister, Dorothy, had stayed there when they visited the Highlands in 1803. We thought we could trust the great romantic poet to lead us to a beautiful place to walk. And so it happened that my first encounter with the unique and peculiar land in the north of Scotland had to be through an Englishman.

We took the train from Edinburgh to the Bridge of Orchy Station. Though it was summer the weather was misty with intermittent rain. I kept my gaze fixed to the window as the train sped through the most captivating land filled with lakes, rivers and waterfalls. I was relishing the ride, not having done much travelling by rail. The opportunity of travelling within Palestine or to the surrounding countries by train had ended in 1948. The establishment of Israel in that year severed the lines of communication between the different parts of the Arab lands in the Levant and beyond it to the Hijaz and North Africa.

It was not a long journey, or so it felt because I was enjoying it so much, and soon we arrived at the station. It was there that I had my first experience of midges, pests the likes of which I had never encountered anywhere else. At first I thought there was something wrong with me. Why was I itching all over my face, neck and hands? I did notice flying around me the flimsiest of creatures; surely they couldn't be responsible. The more I flailed my arms in the air the more they assaulted me. I could stand it no longer. I ran out of the station as fast as I could, dragging my bag behind me pursued by a cloud of irritating midges. Later, after having enjoyed the unspoiled nature of the Highlands, I was not sure whether or not to agree with the Highlander who was grateful for the midges for keeping tourists away. 'Except for them,' he told me, 'tourists would have long since spoiled this place.'

We crossed the Trunk Road and walked over the attractive old bridge. We passed the village where no more than fifteen families live, then followed the asphalted road to the north. We could have taken the dirt path that went straight up Mam Carraigh, but it was only later that we discovered what a pleasant walk this was and how much shorter it would have been than circling the hill on the road. The receptionist had told us the hotel was four miles away from the station. She assumed we would be driving. But neither Penny nor I like to drive. And to rent a car would mean missing the train ride, which we were loath to do. Dragging our bags behind us, we proceeded to walk. The views were gorgeous, especially when we took the final turn around the hill and faced the beautiful Loch Tulla.

Arriving at the hotel, we wasted no time. We climbed the narrow stairs, dropped our bags in a room with a shared bathroom, and rushed out to take our first walk in the Scottish countryside. We were very excited. We had not yet discovered that Ordnance Survey maps are available for all these areas and so could not be adventurous. From a booklet at the hotel we learned that we were near the West Highland Way and that we could walk to the Black Mountain. We decided to use the few hours of daylight left to do this walk.

The moor evoked strong and memorable feelings in me. It appeared to tell of sad stories, to be a place of mystery and danger, though I had no idea why.

It was the first time in my life that I found myself in the middle of a moor. Once there I felt a deep silence descend upon me, unlike any I have known. It was not characterized by the absence of sound, for the moor seemed to breathe, emitting deep sighs as the low wind swept through the water-soaked grass, weeds and bracken. I am used to the silence of the Palestinian hills near Ramallah, my hometown, where I often sit in the shade of a pine tree enjoying the rustle of the wind passing through the fragrant needle leaves. This fitful percussive sound overhead is hardly ever sustained. In contrast, the moan of the wind in the moor is continuous and deep, giving the impression of having travelled long distances to give life to an ancient, desolate terrain. It starts at a lower point, almost level with the ears, sweeping continuously over the flat land, loud then faint then loud again unobstructed by trees. There was sadness in that sound. It was like a wail.

The sweeping of the wind was punctuated only by the sound of water dripping in the undergrowth. The closest landscape to this that I could think of was a glacier with water streaming beneath it which, if one listened intently enough, one could hear. Once while walking in the Swiss Alps I was tempted to trudge over such a glacier. When I later asked a Swiss Italian ski instructor whether it would have been safe to do this, she warned: 'No, no! Crevasses! You fall in and then *finito*.'

Both terrains, the Alpine and the Scottish, and the atmosphere they engendered were unfamiliar to me. Here the colours were muted, so unlike the stark unmitigated glare of the Palestinian hills. The water-saturated air was heavier and fresher, in contrast to the light dry air of the Ramallah hills made fragrant by the numerous herbs that grow there. The clouds moved fast, the sun made brief appearances. When it shone through the thick clouds, the hills were reflected in the lochs. There was more uniformity in our hills, their dry river-beds reflecting nothing.

We can also depend on the weather. For six months of the year we can be certain that no rain will fall. Here in the Highlands the risk of a storm adds to the excitement and the brevity of what can be enjoyed. I could not imagine two landscapes more different than the Scottish and the Palestinian. One stretches open and drenched with water, the other lies fragmented by roads and Jewish settlements and for six months of the year is bone-dry. My lack of familiarity with the moor made me cautious. I could not be sure what would become of me if I were to leave the road and venture into it. Would my unsuspecting feet step on some soft bottomless bog that would suck me down like quicksand in the desert?

My ignorance did not only give rise to such unfounded fears, it also extended to projecting on the land the hardships and danger described in the abridged nineteenth-century novels set in these mysterious lands which my mother used to read to me as we snuggled under the warm quilt in our cold house in Ramallah. The heroine cast out of the manor by the wicked master or stepmother would struggle through the moor (the very word had a mystique), the wind howling, her bare feet scratched by the thick heather, the rain drenching her scanty clothes. In distant Ramallah where no such terrains exist, moors were threatening places. Neither Penny nor I spoke as we trudged on the cobblestones with which this part of the Highland Way was paved, looking with utter fascination at the mysterious countryside around us. The mist was covering most of the fields. Occasionally it would lift and we could see more of the moor with the tobacco-coloured water puddles that reflected the clouds when the sun shone over them.

To our left were mountains. I wondered which one of them was the Black Mountain, and whether it was given this name on account of its colour. In the rain and mist all of them seemed dark to me. The drizzle was getting stronger and soon we would be drenched. We decided to end our first walk into the Scottish Highlands and turn back. As we retraced our path we saw a rainbow that arced down, almost touching the top of the grass in the moor.

At dinner that night we found the hotel's food delicious. Or perhaps it was the walk that had given us so hearty an appetite. In the small dining room five tables were occupied. There was the proverbial father and son who had come on a fishing vacation. The son with the freshness, irony and despair of adolescence looked like he was doing his father a favour by accompanying him. The father was working hard to get his son enthused about the adventures of the next day, talking to him about fishing and its joys. There was no reaction from the son, who seemed only to want the time to pass so that this imposed vacation would come to an end and he could be with his friends again. At a table in the very middle of the room was a stately woman whom the waiter mockingly referred to as The Lady. She was a widow who, as we soon learned, was celebrating on this occasion her eightieth birthday.

We later learned that she was from the seaside town of Helensburgh, and had been coming to this hotel for many years. The sole waiter, a frail man of forty, was utterly drunk yet still managed to put on an air of mock-deference for the benefit of The Lady. Perhaps too much so, bending and bowing in such an exaggerated manner that he ended up spilling food from a serving plate onto the white tablecloth. In her high-handed manner the Lady scolded him. He rushed to the kitchen and came back with a bottle of vintage red wine which he announced was the gift of the management for her birthday. She received it with great style and proceeded to sip from it, becoming more garrulous in the process.

'Where are you walking tomorrow?' The Lady asked Penny.

'In the glen, taking the path along the river.'

'I only like the tops,' The Lady declared. 'My husband, when he was alive, would make it halfway up then I would leave him behind and go up on my own. I'm a woman of the tops,' bragged the old lady, who now could hardly walk.

This ended the conversation. Clearly not being 'people of the tops,' like her, we were deemed unworthy and had fallen in her eyes.

That night we slept well. We had wanted to take a short after-dinner walk, but with the absence of rain the midges were in force. In Ramallah we worry about Israeli soldiers when we think of going out at night; here we had to worry about midges. Both seem to succeed in keeping tourists away. As I turned to sleep the thought came to me that this establishment, its views and sounds, and this land, must have looked and sounded exactly the same as when William and Dorothy Wordsworth visited over two centuries ago. But then I was still ignorant of the immense changes that had befallen the land and its inhabitants since that time.

'Careful, the plate is very hot,' warned the buxom woman who was serving our breakfast and whom we had not seen at dinner. I ordered the full Scottish vegetarian breakfast and ate every morsel. I felt totally fortified for a long walk. Before breakfast I had gone out and seen the low mist over the nearby loch, but now I could see from the window that it was lifting and to my utter surprise a few rays of sunlight had managed to infiltrate the clouds. I had begun to think it was boycotting Scotland.

As the matronly waitress was picking up the dirty plates I struck up a conversation. It began with the kinds of dogs her family owned. I was surprised when she said they had five shepherd dogs.

'Why so many?' I asked.

'To handle the sheep. My husband has five hundred of them,'

she proudly announced.

'Then you must be rich,' I said.

'O no! They're not ours. My husband is just the shepherd.'

It was this woman's passing comment that induced me to read more about the history of the Highlands and learn about the great tragedy that had afflicted the people living there in the eighteenth and early nineteenth centuries, leaving behind those ghosts with their many stories waiting to be heard.

A year later we came back to Glen Orchy for another walking vacation. This time the weather was kinder to us. And what a difference the sun made!

It was as though I was venturing into a transformed land, not the same terrain that I had walked in a year ago in drizzle and storm. The water in the Kinglass River was no longer rushing in the harried manner it had done then. It was as though idling to catch more of the sun. I stopped at Victoria Bridge and looked at the water. I could see the spray as the water hit the rocks playfully reaching out, sparkling in the clear air. Even the sound of the full flowing river was not the same. On our earlier visit it had sounded rushed and turbulent; today it flowed with a soothing ripple as if it were murmuring contentedly. In the clear, bright light I had a full view of shimmering Loch Tulla stretching luxuriously through the grassy moor with a stately estate by its side, and a tiny island floating near the middle shaded by a single tree evoking a world of quiet repose.

We took the road we had walked earlier to get to the West Highland Way, and just before turning left at the house with the garden we had to step aside to allow the 4X4 jeep to pass. It was on its way to the estate by the loch, which we later learned belonged to the Fleming family who claim Ian, the creator of the James Bond books, as an illustrious son. We now turned west and started on the Old Military Road. Walking by the cultivated forest, the River Kinglass ran to our left. It was wider here and flowed slowly. Its shallow bed was full of shiny round stones. I stopped to take in the view. What superb country this is. The river flowed in an open expansive glen with hills to the north, and along our path as far as the eye could see lay more lochs with a track that would take days to traverse.

I thought of Palestine's main river, the Jordan, and how it was impossible to take such a walk along its banks, for the river is caged in barbed wire from the point where it leaves Lake Tiberius until it flows into the Dead Sea. The smooth contours of the green hills here reminded me of the Galilee hills in spring. Not long ago I walked in them searching for the villages that a great-great-uncle of mine used as hiding places when he was on the run to escape arrest by Ottoman forces during the First World War. Those villages were all destroyed in 1948 when Israel was established. Cleared of its former inhabitants, the land is now used to plant barley and wheat. I had tried to imagine what it must have been like over sixty years ago when it was alive with the labour of simple farmers, their lowing animals and active village life. Now the land lay silent except for the whisper of the wind among the wheat stalks. A silence not unlike the quiet pervading these Highlands which, as I now know, had been inhabited until the early nineteenth century when greedy landlords decided it was more profitable to raise sheep and forced the tenants out of the land.

In his book, *The Crofter and the Laird,* John McPhee describes the houses of these clansmen:

> *'[They] were called black houses, because peat was burned in them in open fires on hearthstones set in the middle of dirt floors, and the peat smoke seeped out through various holes in the thatch above after coating*

the interior of the house with smudge. Cattle and horses lived in the houses, too, or in adjacent byres. The animals often used the same entrance the people used. Windows were not glazed. When cold winds were blowing, the windows were stuffed with sod.'

To the landlords who wanted the land without its people these black houses must have seemed worthless. They demolished them to induce people to leave, thus ending a whole way of life. The same happened in the Galilee. And just as the Victorian pilgrims to the Holy Land failed to see the Arab inhabitants, when these fine folk came to paint the Highlands they used the deer as a symbol of the land, calling it the Monarch of the Glen. They preferred an empty land which they could use as a sporting playground and a romantic wilderness. In Scotland the action of the landlords has changed the land forever, but has not torn it asunder and brought in new inhabitants to populate it, as happened in Palestine – where in the Galilee hills I now walk as a stranger, a tourist in the land that had once belonged to my forefathers.

The history of people and their land cannot be separated. Some lands, like Palestine and Scotland, bear the scars of what was done to the people inhabiting them. Walking there can evoke those painful memories. In the Galilee hills I try to read the few remaining traces of what once was: stones piled in a certain way, a cistern dug in the earth, fruit trees growing in a field of clover. All speak of the trauma experienced by those who once inhabited those hills. I tried to do the same in the Highlands.

As I am all too well aware from the *Nakba,* as the mass eviction of the Arabs from Palestine in 1948 is called, monumental events like these do not only have political and social consequences. They affect the very soul of the nation. They are passed on like DNA from one generation to another, for it appears that nations who have suffered great injustices share the mixed blessing of a long memory. I have spent many years trying to analyse the effect of the *Nakba* on the consciousness of my people. I wonder what effect the Clearances had on the consciousness of the Scottish people. I cannot experience these glens in the Highlands without thinking of this question. Many a large and beautiful glen has not always been devoid of inhabitants, the number of sheep far exceeding that of humans. Having cleared away the people, the heartless new owners of the land brought in hundreds of thousands of sheep to replace them. These came to be known by the few who stayed as 'the four-legged lairds.' In some places where ten thousand people once lived, the only remaining inhabitants now live in twenty or thirty houses. Landowners acted upon the belief that their lands would be more profitable inhabited by sheep rather than people, and so the people had to go. Heart-wrenching scenes have been described of the long marches that many of these Highlanders had to take to get to the beaches. There they had to fend for themselves without shelter or food. They were mountain folk and did not know the ways of the sea. Many a Scottish woman was widowed as the men perished in seafaring adventures that they were ill-equipped to handle.

In Palestine there was movement in the opposite direction. The inhabitants of the coastal towns of Lyda and Ramleh were forced out by the Israeli army in 1948. Thousands of Palestinians were forced to walk eastward under the July sun, at first dropping belongings and later leaving bodies of men, women and children scattered along the way. The anger felt as new generations learn of that embittering history seems not to diminish with time.

In Palestine the lamb is a symbol of peace and love. I have always found the sight of flocks being shepherded in the hills pleasing. I wonder how these sheep must be seen by the locals here. Does the prejudice remain, two centuries after the humans were replaced by these complacent and often foolish animals? In the mid-eighteenth century even the wearing of tartan cloth was banned by an Act of Parliament enacted at Westminster. Through other Acts the clansmen were disarmed and the seven-hundred-year era of regional government by the clan system was ended forever, just like the leadership of local tribesmen was ended in the hills of the Galilee. What remains now is the nostalgia expressed by what to me is the strange sight of men wearing kilts embossed with badges and coats-of-arms that have no relationship to present reality. But invented traditions that are not rooted in a viable way of life cannot be satisfying. Their lustre soon fades. As is the case in Scotland, the people of Palestine also hold on to folklore, which in many cases echoes the rural lifestyle of communities in the parts of Palestine lost to Israel.

Palestine and Scotland also share similarities in the way it became possible for some of the villagers to become disposable tenants. In nineteenth-century Palestine the Ottomans introduced a new land code that made it possible for the first time in the history of the country to register land. Absentee landowners who could afford the fees and regarded land as an investment registered large tracts in their name. One single family in Beirut came to own the land of seventy villages in Palestine's great plain, Marj Ibn Amer. This severed the traditional bond between landowner and tenant. Likewise in Scotland after the Battle of Culloden: even where clan chiefs continued to hang on to their lands, they were stripped of their powers over their tenants. The villagers in both Palestine and Scotland came to have no protection.

In Palestine when Zionist colonisers offered large sums to these absentee landowners, some of them agreed to sell and the tenants who had lived all their lives on the land were evicted. In Scotland's Highlands the lairds sold out to men from the lowlands and England. The small farm society that had evolved in the glens was wiped out. It took the war of 1948 in Palestine to complete the process of destroying and depopulating 418 villages. In the more than sixty years since that event took place the part of Palestine that became Israel went through an almost total transformation. The country was changed to fit an image that the mainly east European Jews who were in control tried to impose on it. To emulate the West, large public gardens were cultivated with lawns that could only be kept green by using the most precious resource of the land, water. The excessive pumping of water from the underground aquifers without allowing these to replenish has forced us all to live under the shadow of the looming disaster of drought.

Unlike the Scottish Clearances (the very word, which came into use long after the events it describes, is offensive – implying that human beings can be 'cleared' like weeds or rubble) Palestine's *Nakba* took place during the lifetime of a generation that is still alive today. But time is not the only factor. The wrenching past lives on in the national consciousness of both people. Two hundred years later many of the descendants of the Highlanders who were evicted yearn for the land out of which their forefathers were forced and the way of life that has ceased to exist there, as attested by the number of histories, novels and plays about these events still being written in Scotland and amongst immigrant communities in North America and Australia.

As I was beginning to get carried away with the resemblances in history and nature between the land I grew up in and this Scottish land, I reached the top of Aonach Eagach. The Lady would be proud of me. I had assumed that one would only be able to see more hill tops from that high vantage point. But ahead of me there was yet another lochan, one that seemed so idyllic, couched in the cusp of the hill fed by a small river that then left it to proceed further to another glen and another loch.

It lay there, silent and remote, a place on which I could project other thoughts and feelings and test myself against what was remote enough for me to represent the wild. Palestine/Israel is too small to have places of real escape like this. In the Highlands the loss of that way of life was not replaced by another. The landlords who evicted the farmers did not bring their own people to replace them. The land returned to what it had been: empty glens, rivers and lochs offering hikers a superb view of an exquisite land that seems to be there for their sole enjoyment.

This beautiful land spread before me. I thought of the many ways in which the history of my people in Palestine makes me angry and, without a solution in sight, continues to be a source of fury. Even as I walk I carry so much baggage that wears me out and weighs me down. All along the way in this beautiful glen and up these hills I had been identifying and unburdening myself of one cause of anger after another arising from the effect of living under a foreign occupation in a land that was becoming out of reach to the non-Jewish inhabitants. Along the path I continued to shed them, so that by the time I reached the top of this hill, panting and short of breath, I felt that I had disposed of so much of the baggage I had been carrying that when I finally paused to rest, breathing deeply, I felt light-headed and unburdened. The long climb had helped chase the angry thoughts away.

As I stood there relieved and refreshed I thought of what Robert Macfarlane wrote in *The Wild Places:* 'We are fallen in mostly broken pieces, but the wild can still return us to ourselves.' Over the years I have returned to the Highlands to do exactly that.

The Road North

Judith Thurley

I invite you to leave your stuffy workplace, pack your rucksack, put on your boots and come with me. It becomes ever more challenging to find truly wild and remote places this far north in Ireland but search we will, for the sake of our sanity, our health and our spiritual well-being.

We might walk Whitepark Bay on the Sea of Moyle, where the Children of Lir were banished by their aunt and stepmother Aoife to spend five hundred years as swans on these turbulent waters. This thunderous sparkling place dwarfs us with its energy. Something in the way the land sweeps down from low cliff to dunes to meet the roar of the Atlantic, tears at my heart. This is a dangerous yet exquisitely beautiful meeting-place of the elements of water, earth and air, and yet something not quite seen seems to take refuge, to nest, in the curve of the land. It was of this place that songwriter Martin Donnelly wrote: *Did I feel the angels' wings? I really cannot say, but something touched my living soul when we walked Whitepark Bay.* It was here that I heard the voice of my friend Marian Bellew, one-time Buddhist nun, who was on her sickbed in Glastonbury, urging me to dance, to dance; where I unabashedly danced sevens and jig-steps on the sand, to discover on returning home that she had succumbed to her cancer and died that day. Just to sit or to walk here becomes pure meditation. Sand reveals itself as a gift, a martyrdom of stone and shell down a million years. Gratitude for such self-sacrifice from the humble pebble awakens some slumbering part of my heart. Sit all day if you want to on this smooth rock and feel your heart pummelled by the impact and roar of the arching waves.

Look – there is the ruin of the old youth hostel, where my

parents and their friends spent their weekends in the years immediately after the Second World War, as a young, eager work party, painting and mending the building.

Now let's move on, because the cattle walking the sands, the new youth hostel under the hill, the houses on the clifftop and the sign warning of the danger of swimming here are too many reminders of human presence. To find somewhere wild, let's go northwest to Malin Head on Inis Eoighan (Inishowen) peninsula in Donegal, the northernmost point in Ireland. To reach Malin Head we travel west from the village of Malin and take the road along the northern shore of Trawbreaga Bay. Already I feel the excitement of homecoming. It is as if happiness runs through my veins. It is beautiful here, a place which I turn to frequently in the world of my imagination; a place governed by light and colour; specifically turquoise and gold. Home to heron and redshank, Brent goose, shelduck and other waders, this part of God's Earth nourished my soul as a child and nurtured my imagination. Its threads of moss, grasses, rock, sand, sky and ocean were woven into the fabric of my very being, of the person I am now. Like the mountains we will visit later, I thirst after this place when I am away, and feast on it when I can make the pilgrimage to be here.

At low tide you might imagine that you could walk across the sand and then wade the narrow channel of water left in this wide inlet. Every Sunday young John Davis, of the Davis's farm on the shore road, rowed across to have dinner with a friend on Doagh Isle, not really an isle at all but a peninsula, tantalisingly close, and easier to reach by boat than by road. John Davis died much too young, killed neither by sea nor by storm, but by his own tractor which rolled over as he laboured to farm this boggy land. On out the road, the meaning of Trawbreaga, *tra bhreige* becomes clear: *treacherous strand.* The inlet is extremely narrow at its mouth – just a few hundred yards across – and the tide races in and out here at Lagg at shocking speed. Out to sea, what looks like a standing wave, a wall of white water, can be seen where this narrow channel meets the full force of the Atlantic. On round the curve of the shore, on Five Fingers Strand, the bones of the wreck of the Twilight, a sailing ship from 1889, are visible at low tide. But be wary if you succumb to the temptation to walk out to the wreck: these sands are unstable and the tide swirls and rushes in unpredictably and erratically. Only the foolhardy or the suicidal swim here, surrendering themselves to the thundering breakers and fierce currents.

Once out on Banba's Crown, the tip of Malin Head, you will be further north than any other person in Ireland. To the west is proud Fanad Head thrusting out into the ocean, and beyond, layer upon layer of headlands fading into charcoal and indigo in the distant mist and spray, and finally the silhouette of Tory Island. In front of you, five miles offshore is the island of Inistrahull and beyond her, the Tor Rocks. Here, I have startled and been startled by the brown hare leaping up and bolting from his heathery bed. If the weather is soft it is beautiful and benign, but it is so exposed that there are often gales. It is bleak and bereft of trees, and often I have felt at the mercy of the wind. In gale-force winds the blue-green Atlantic swell can quickly be transformed into mountainous murky grey waves, which seem to threaten to swallow the whole headland. I adore it but I fear it too, and if I am honest perhaps it is that intermingling of beauty and danger which pulls me back here again and again, some unconscious recognition of my ancestry and a merging of that awe and dread of the ocean which lies deep in the psyche and the soul of the island dweller. In the sixth century, when Ireland was sparsely populated, covered in wild woodland and bog, and unpolluted but for turfsmoke and woodsmoke, Columcille, the great early Christian abbot, wrote the following verses:

Delightful I think it to be in the bosom of an isle,
on the crest of a rock,
that I may look there on the manifold
face of the sea.

That I may see its heavy waves
over the glittering ocean
as they chant a melody to their Father
on their eternal course

... That contrition of heart should come upon me
when I look upon it;
that I may bewail my many sins
difficult to declare.

Columcille might have been writing about Lough Foyle, only a few miles from here. In these lines we can get a sense of the respect our ancestors had for the ocean. Columcille saw himself as part of the natural world humbly joining in the chorus already begun by the elements and he tells us that time spent by the sea can bring a calming of the inner tumult. Maharishi Mahesh Yogi advised his devotees that water absorbs stress, that to sit or walk beside a body of water would bring physiological and spiritual healing. This is a far cry from the words of Tibetan mystic and poet Nyoshul Khen Rinpoche: 'Rest in natural great peace this exhausted mind, beaten helpless by karma and neurotic thought, like the relentless fury of the pounding waves, in the infinite ocean of Samsara.' On a calm day, I might question his vision of the ocean as a simile for samsara, or suffering, but up here even in summer; or in winter, during a storm which lasts say, three days, with only five or six hours of daylight and little respite from the shriek of gale and roar of waves, I do of course experience that relentless fury to which he refers, as a negative force.

Look behind you, my friend: there is the ruin of the Lloyd's signal station and though it offers shelter from the ever-present wind, its history does not justify its ugliness nor its stubborn presence, and almost everywhere we walk on Malin Head we are thwarted by someone's love of fences, making it difficult to get off the road. I will sit down in the lee of the rocks and play a few jigs and reels on the whistle, followed by a slow air, *Lament for the Wild Salmon,* and then let's move on. Perhaps to find wilderness we must go to an island: Rathlin, with its deafening population of puffins, guillemots, razorbills and kittiwakes, just six miles off the Antrim coast and only fifteen miles from the Mull of Kintyre. Or Tory Island where you can still hear the corncrakes in early summer; or Aranmore, further west round the Donegal coast.

First though, let's travel southwest to the sea cliffs of Slieve League in South Donegal, *where silence roars like the wind.* We might take half a day to clamber from the village of Carrick up the landward slopes to the summit, and lie on our bellies, peering over the edge to look straight down on steeply sloping grassy fields, and below them the waves crashing into the base of the cliffs 2000 feet beneath us. All the hues and shades of greens, blues, turquoise and crystalline white are created in the churning waters and their beauty takes my breath away. But this too is a dangerous place. The weather can change quickly and people have lost their lives here just from a slip of the foot. Let's move on again, as we can see from up here the car park where those less able or willing than us, or those with less time, have driven part-way to the top and today we do not wish for so much company.

We go east now, to the coast of County Down and the Mourne Mountains. We will take two walks: the first a gentle walk along the Ott track which traverses Ott mountain. Ott is a low hill whose original Irish name Ocht means breast.

This feels significant, for it recognises the mountain as place of nourishment: in summer, to lie on the heather gazing out at the infinite blue of the sky, is to nestle on the bosom of the Mother. The rough path climbs gently. It is March and you can see clumps of frogspawn in the streams and flooded places. Let's pause to bless new life, lying here vulnerable and trusting. The sheep are down off the hills for lambing, so once we leave the Fofanny Bane Road behind us, it is unusually silent. Not even a raven. Just the wind – the sound of the very air itself moving; the crunch and squelch of our bootsteps on stone or moss, and our own breathing. It is good to remember that last summer, a landslide blocked that road, taking trees and dry stone walls in its path, and changing the shape of the hill forever. The road was closed for days, if not weeks. It caused our small convoy of furniture removal van and two cars, as we attempted to move house from North to South Down, to turn back and pick our way along sodden narrow by-roads through the mountains. It is good to be reminded sometimes that nature cannot be tamed as easily as we might like. Personally, I enjoyed being thwarted and unexpectedly put in my place that day, and the 'dramatic-ness' of it outweighed the inconvenience.

Not so very far from here is one of the huts where I spent many childhood weekends with my family, immersed in the sights, sounds and smells of the hills. 'The Hut' was home of the Slievadore Club, a mountaineering club founded by my father and a group of friends. It was a small farmhouse, two-up, two-down, with no electricity and a well some yards down the road where we children were sent for the water. We learned how to dress properly for walking in the mountains, and how to walk at the pace of the slowest (or youngest) member of the group, and we learned rock climbing and abseiling. I loved the racket and camaraderie at the end of a day's walking, all those towering grown-ups in their corduroy breeks and brushed cotton shirts, their thick red socks and huge clumping boots. Someone would light the fire and 'get the pan on' and enamel mugs of tea would be passed round, and later, mugs of hot whiskey, and then of course the songs would start.

Now let's push on up to the Mourne Wall where we can shelter from the wind, and eat. Carn Mountain is on our right and Slieve Lough Shannagh rises to our left, and beyond her, Slievemeelmore and Sleivemeelbeg. Before us, Doan, all moss-stitch, quiver of bog-cotton and grey granite, and below her the mysterious presence of Lough Shannagh. Today's fall of snow lies on the tops of the hills. I look up and marvel at the pale blue-whiteness of the sky and the mistiness of the clouds, higher now that the snowstorm has moved away eastwards. I think of the Spanish word *niebla* for mist, how it is related to the English word *nebulous*. I say both words to myself, gazing at the sky, and I realise that there is no word to describe the sky this particular evening, that it is somewhere between the nebulousness of mist and the milky melt-water of a glacier. Then I see the pale risen moon over the mountains and I am quiet.

There is one more place I would show you. Slieve Donard, our highest mountain, rises straight up out of the Irish Sea where the Glen River completes its short journey. We climb beside boulders, pools and waterfalls using the ancient tree roots as steps and relishing the pungent scent of mixed woodland. I will resist the urge to swim in the many enticing basins and pools on the way up until we reach the exact pool that waits for us. It is long, narrow and wonderfully deep, accessible by a clamber off the track and over boulders at the lower end, and only by a high dive or jump at the top end. I am no diver. It is well worth the *sprauchle* over the slippery boulders to immerse yourself in the freezing crystal-clear water. This is a pure and primal experience: a cold bath, a baptism; a surrendering:

I plunge and swim in water come down
from under ground above me;
belly of Donard and Commedagh.
The April river is melted snow,
clear as light. I yelp with cold,
swim under hanging rhododendron
to the moss-cushioned waterfall.

I circle the green pool.

The world is all water crystal light,
all river mountain sky,
and I am goatfish woman:
horn, hoof and fish's tail.
I climb mountains, clamber upwards:
find what I yearn for in the waters
of a green river pool.
I plunge and swim and sing a prayer
that every child, woman and man
in all the round reaches
of the sighing world
will find a clear green pool
to swim in.

I have swum in the river in every season, even at Christmas when I don't stay long in the water. But when I wrote 'Goatfish Woman' it was a cold snowy April and I wondered if I would make it back down the mountain. I had come unprepared for a swim, but allowed myself to be coaxed in by the enthusiasm of another walker who was already on his descent. As he declared passionately 'I can't go past it! I can't go past it!' he wheaked off his clothes and in he went. I knew just what he meant. I followed suit, swimming in my underwear, but I stayed in longer than he did. As I got used to the cold I wanted to stay in the river forever. When at last I talked myself into getting out of the water, I realised that I had started to lose my coordination. With no towel, I struggled to dress myself, and eventually stumbled back down through the forest, with double vision and my body shuddering. It took several hours, extra layers of clothes and numerous hot drinks before I recovered.

So today, yes, we might swim in the river, but we will come out in good time and warm ourselves with a drink of hot soup and then we will climb on up Donard. Donard can feel like a difficult climb, partly because it begins at sea-level, but mostly because of her false summit. Once on top, however, there is the sparkling Irish Sea before you as your trophy. Rest. Catch your breath. Turn around slowly, taking in the view of this small range of mountains from the top of its highest peak; in perfect weather you can see the Blue Stack mountains in Donegal, Scafell in Cumbria, Snaefell on the Isle of Man, Snowdon, and even Slieve Bloom to the south. To sit up here and gaze mindfully upon a granite boulder, or on this tiny star-flower; or to glimpse a world within a gurgling underground spring whose doorway is draped with a bejewelled spider's web; or simply to sit beside a stream letting the harmony of its voice wash over us, is the beginning of healing.

Now let's lift a stone and leave our small mark by placing it on the cairn before we walk back down over the grass and boulders, through the forest, restored by the spirit of the mountain and the hurtling river, back down to our other lives...

Come dusk I'll cry no more;
the mountain breathes forgiveness,
the voice of Love is flawless.

Whale Song

Lesley Harrison

I am very lucky to live right on the coast, and am always at some level aware of the sea behind my house. The North Sea has its own colour palette, a range of shades from white to blue and grey that are never silent. On the one side of me there are fields, cottages, lanes, trees and hills. On the other, a great volume of space and light that is continually emptying and filling with sound: the sounds of geese, grass, cloud, wind ... the very sounds of colour changing.

Our part of the coast was formed when Scotland lay south of the Equator. The climate was hot and very dry, and huge rivers flowed across the arid landscape leaving layers of sand and silt and gravel which, over millions of years, compacted to form a pebbly red sandstone. Over time the river bed tilted out of the sea, cracking and sliding downhill, forming buttresses and blow holes. Now prehistoric caves rounded out by deeper currents gape high overhead. You walk among the tide wrack beneath overhanging shelves and ledges, each its own shade of ochre and studded with multi-coloured, egg-shaped stones. These, which we collect for our gardens and patios, were rounded and smoothed by a warm saliva sea over 400 million years ago.

It was several months after I moved here that I realised that the upturned boat slowly mouldering away was actually the carcass of a small whale. A humpback whale, in fact; an infant. A winter storm left it on a small ridge of sand and pebble at the foot of a steep, brambly slope. At very high tides the waves can just reach it. Depending on the swell, it sometimes sits proud of the beach on a pedestal of stones; at other times it is almost completely covered over.

Millions of years ago, a group of mammals left dry land and

walked back into the water. Their tails turned into huge flukes; their legs disappeared into their sides. Now they move in an entirely different universe, a world with its own unimaginable depths and levels, its own time sequences, its own weight and colour.

The first thing a newborn whale hears is singing.

The idea of the Earth producing music comes from a time when the sun, moon and stars were thought to revolve round the Earth in concentric orbits. Mediaeval astronomers were looking for evidence of design in the organisation and structure of the world, and believed they could find examples of the beautiful structures of music in planetary movements. These were men of the church, who devoted themselves to thought and conducted their investigations between its offices, who lived among psalms and plainsongs with phrases which rose and lasted as long as a breath. The unearthly beauty of the harmonies in music, they said, could not possibly have been man-made. These were an observable result of intelligent design. The perfect matching of notes to produce chords; the subtle, geometric accuracy of shifts of pitch and key; this was proof of God's ability to create perfection. And what was Earth but an imperfect copy of God's perfect creation, the heavens? In their maps of the skies, therefore, each planet was separated from its neighbours by harmonic intervals: just as music follows regular patterns in octaves, chords and melodies, so they looked for such spacings in their astronomical measurements and observations. Some did actually believe the heavens produced sound as the spheres rotated. Boethius called it 'musica mundana', the 'natural music of the world'. It is inaudible to us, he said, because of our inherent physical imperfection. Our own music, that which we make ourselves with our voices and instruments, was 'musica instrumentalis ... a poorer, tangible form of that which is unknowable to us.'

Mediaeval thinkers clung to this idea despite growing evidence to the contrary. Tycho Brahe's instruments hugely increased the accuracy of measurements of planetary movements, and he rewrote the model of concentric spheres to fit the data. His pupil Johannes Kepler improved Brahe's telescopes and checked and revised his tables, producing far more accurate observations which he then went to immense lengths to match to the architecture of music. In *Harmonies of the World* he describes how positions of certain bodies in the night sky mirror points on the musical scale, their movements matching major and minor keys, thirds and fifths in chords and so on. One chapter is called *The Universal Harmonies of All Six Planets may Exist, like Common Quadriform Counterpoint;* another *In the Celestial Concords Which Planet sings Soprano, Which Alto, Which Tenor and Which Bass.* For Kepler, geometry and harmony had a single source, and he saw incontrovertible evidence of both when he looked at the night sky.

All whales produce melodic sounds, the pitch and volume depending on the size of the whale. Whales play for three times longer than they hunt, creating huge extended games that range right across the ocean. Humpbacks can swim at up to 50mph, subtly altering the shape of their bodies to slip between layers of current and glide without friction in weightless space. They dive a mile down, dropping their heart beat, collapsing their lungs to adjust to the greater pressure; they use the rotation of the planet, magnetic and lunar currents and the contours of the seabed to find their way south to mate. Once the calf is born, it needs to be exposed to air before its blow hole opens and it begins to breathe. Its mother nudges it to the surface, and helps it learn to swim.

The song of the blue whale is said to be like being in an earth tremor. As far as we know, whales sing mostly during the winter breeding season when they congregate in the same specific breeding grounds. Only the males sing. For a long time it was assumed to be sexual behaviour to attract females, who do not sing. However, no one has ever seen a female humpback show any interest in the song. Also, when humpback males sing, they usually suspend themselves motionless underwater in a curved posture, in a kind of trance. A lone whale might hang in the darkness, sing continuously to himself, for days.

Philosophers argue long and hard about what is beautiful, or meaningful, in music. The functionalist says music is one way of including the individual in a community. Music is an affective language: it produces feelings of recognition or self-knowledge in us. Its structure, and any other recognisable qualities, are created within a culture. The pleasure we experience listening to music is the joy of recognition. A song is no more nor less than its significance to, and effect on, the listener.

Yet often the sense of longing that we feel when we listen to 'beautiful' music is unearthly, beyond words. We can be surprised by the same sense of abandonment, the same feeling of wordless awe, when listening to symphonies and counterpoints or a single human voice, or birdsong, or waves. I am always struck dumb by winter geese flying overhead, and the urgent croaking of the cantor, neck out, high up in the sunset. It is the same feeling I get sitting alone late in the evening, listening to one particular piece of music, as the other instruments fall away and leave the violin rising and falling alone in the dark. The most beautiful music renders us speechless.

When the tide is at its lowest, the fishermen go down to the shore and set up their lines. In winter, the landscape is drab, with only local boils of colour: lichen burnt on stone; the purple black of buckthorn; yellow gorse lights, red oilskins. These solitary figures spend hours standing in silence, watching the sea. When you stand on the beach you can see grey water piling towards you, higher than your head. Closer in are submerged rocks whose black amorphic forms loom to the surface as the sea sinks. At low tide, they foam and spout, blowing spray high into the air, water pouring down their sides. The beach is strewn with boulders carved into odd shapes, like vertebrae or knuckle bones.

The first warning of bad weather is usually the rafts of duck and seagulls floating close in, mute and folded. From the top of the cliff you can see burst clouds hanging offshore, heavy watery blues and purples flattening the sea beneath them. The storms that hurl down the coast are truly impressive; howling between the houses like banshees, churning salt water into the air. Waves topple towards the cliffs trapping air that is released like an explosion against the rock face, bursting holes like fistula, throwing pebbles up into the fields.

Over time, as the whale decomposed, its colours and textures changed, the sun and rain burning their own colours into its skin. By January, its outer layer was a beautiful rusted felt, fibrous and combed like sheep's wool. Lines of tiny stones lay like jewellery where the skin sagged between ribs. Its spine was lumpy and protruding, its mouth full of pebbles.

In his 1854 book *The Beautiful in Music*, Peter Hanslick said that music, like language, consists of organized sounds, but unlike language, those sounds have no referent. He says: 'in music there is both language and logical sequence, but in a musical sense; it is language we speak and understand, but which we are unable to translate.' Its aesthetic value ('the beautiful') lies in 'the ingenious co-ordination of intrinsically pleasing sounds, their consonance and contrast, their flight and reproach, their increasing and diminishing strength ...'

One feature of whale music which excites real awe among whale watchers is the way in which songs are shared over vast distances. A pattern 'sung' by one lone whale will be repeated less than an hour later by another on the other side of the ocean. The song of the humpback also evolves as it is shared between individuals, and changes in one region are mimicked almost immediately among other groups hundreds of miles away. Song patterns that evolved and were then broken off one season will be picked up and continued years later.

Unlike nearly all bird songs, a humpback whale's song constantly changes during the breeding season. Humpback songs are far more musical in structure than the sound of any other dolphin or whale. They live and migrate in more accessible parts of the ocean, and so their sounds are relatively easy to record. Biologists have made many attempts to record and analyse their songs which, they say, seem to be made up of repeating patterns, hierarchically organized around phrases. Some believe they have identified phrases which end with the same contrasting sound, like rhymed verse. Recurring elements and patterns seem to be carried on between individuals, then dropped, then picked up again months later in entirely different parts of the ocean. Whales seem to draw these phrases from a living collective memory thousands, possibly millions, of years old.

Marine biologists monitoring humpbacks in their breeding grounds off central America note the following: when a new pattern appears in a song, the other males strive to copy the new element and in a matter of weeks all are singing the same new song. In birds, widely separated populations tend to have different 'dialects' in their songs, but widely dispersed humpback whales often have the same song, and they change it together, in tandem.

One theory is that they use thermoclines, which are layers of warmer or cooler water between which sound can be reflected like an echo continually bouncing off parallel walls. By sinking to these layers, it appears whales can call to each other, even across an ocean. Great strings of music are hung across the darkness. Their whole body senses the song; they feel the music with the surface of their skin, in the movement of their bones, in the corridors of their bodies. They make the sound for a distant, invisible audience, and the sound travels through them.

Twentieth-century composers developed the idea of the autonomous, non-referential character of music in ways which go against the traditional idea of music as harmonious, or 'euphonic'. One early exponent was the poet Ezra Pound who composed pieces in which, he said, the rhythm carried the meaning. He used 'the rhythms of the human body' – in fact, one score calls for human bones to be used for percussion – with scratches, hiccoughs and other counter-rhythms. Going in another direction, John Cage celebrated the role of silence in composition by setting aside four minutes, thirty-three seconds for audience and performer to listen together to the space and emptiness surrounding them.

Though much mocked, he was demonstrating a truth known to the mediaeval astronomers: in plainsongs, the silences are equally pure. A conductor holds the audience and orchestra still for a moment at the beginning and the end of a performance, giving us time to cross the No-Man's Land between here-and-now and this other world that music creates. When we are lost in a piece of music, we are completely alone.

Now at the end of its fifth winter, all that remains of the whale is a rough imprint on the beach, like a silhouette cut out of brownish tarpaulin, roughly the shape of a whale. It has almost completely sunk back into the earth.

One night in December when the sky was all but empty save

for the ashes of the sunset, I went out along the cliffs. When it is completely dark it is impossible to distinguish between earth and sky: the lights from the ships appear low down or high up in the darkness depending on how far out they are at sea. The lighthouse, thirteen miles out, flashes near the foot of Orion. A shooting star might be a flare from an oil rig. You realise you are standing on a ledge at the very brink of the universe. The depth, the sheer volume of all that darkness, suddenly flow towards and over you like an ocean.

In 1893, Fritjof Nansen and his crew set off on the *Fram* to determine the extent of land round the North Pole. They anchored themselves to the sea ice and let it freeze around them. Then, using the movements of the planets, they measured their slow, circular drift, plotting the sea-bed and the cooler and warmer layers of water beneath them. They discovered the denser saline currents which flowed into the Arctic basin from the Atlantic and sank under the warmer, less briny water of the Polar Sea. Amid all his hydrographic and meteorological observations, his charts and tables, accounts and inventories compiled during the three years he was frozen in, Nansen allows himself occasional moments of revery. On 26th September 1894, he looked up and considered 'the unknowable': 'Nothing more wonderfully beautiful can exist than the arctic night. It is dreamland, painted in the imagination's most delicate tints; it is colour etherialised. One shade melts into the other, so that you cannot tell where one ends and the other begins, and yet they are all there. No forms – it is all faint, dreamy colour music, a far-away, long-drawn-out melody on muted strings.'

Should we be looking for similarities between human and whale music? As a thought-experiment it is flawed from the outset: we know we produce music self-consciously, mimicking the sounds we have been surrounded by since birth. Our traditions have grown up through collective effort and consensus over hundreds, or thousands, of years. How can we look for similarities in the noises produced by completely different species whose consciousness, whose experience and whose collective memory will always be to us entirely unknown, and unknowable? We yearn for points of contact; we too can be lost to ourselves in the beauty of a piece of music. We can long for the depth and the secrecy of the sea; we envy what we think of as their purity of thought. But we are separate, by millions of years.

Peter Matthiessen, in *Blue Meridian,* says: 'No word conveys the eeriness of the whale song, tuned by the ages to a purity beyond refining, a sound that man should hear each morning to remind him of the morning of the world.' Voyager I and II, in their endless journey out from Earth, have in their cargoes recordings of whale sounds as a sound picture of life on our planet.

Nansen describes the aurora borealis as a 'symphony of infinitude. I have never been able to grasp the fact that the Earth will one day be spent and desolate and empty. To what end, then, all this beauty, with not a creature to rejoice in it? Now I begin to divine it – this is the coming Earth. Here are beauty and death. But to what purpose? Ah, to what purpose all these spheres? Read the answer, if you can, in the starry blue firmament.'

Bibliography

Seay, Albert. *Music in the Medieval World* Prentice Hall, 1965. 2nd ed. (History of Music)

Hanslick, Peter. *The Beautiful in Music* Kessinger, 1854

Nansen, Fritjof. *Farthest north* Birlinn, 2002

Matthiessen, Peter. *Blue meridian : the search for the great white shark* Penguin, 1971

Strata

Sara Maitland

There are three main sorts of rock: igneous, metamorphic and sedimentary rocks.

Sedimentary rocks are easily the smallest group on the planet overall, nonetheless between 70% and 80% of the rocks we see, the surface rocks, are sedimentary. Erosion, by wind, water and chemical process, breaks up the mother rock and carries it somewhere else and lays it down in a flat layer. Then pressure, or heat, or some other processes cause lithification: the layer of sediment is turned into a layer of solid rock. Often another layer is laid on top of that, and then another, like slices of bread in a loaf. Sometimes these layers, or strata as they are called, are themselves eroded, mixed and re-lithified; sometimes they are warped, lifted or broken up; sometimes the older original rock breaks through the layers. But whatever happens, sedimentary rocks are the texts of pre-history; however far they are pushed or moved they will contain information about where they came from. From them we learn where the land and the oceans once were. Anything that is going to be fossilised is fossilised in sedimentary rocks. We know about sea levels, about temperature, about the weather, and about emerging life-forms from sedimentary rocks. You look at the strata – what is in each of them and their relationship to each other – and, if you have the knowledge, you can see the silent history of the wild silent places.

Geology is a long, slow process. But something not dissimilar happens on the surface too. You take any place, and time rolls across it, laying down layers of sediment. These layers shift and warp and sometimes you can see several strata at once, poking up from underneath each other, breaking into sight.

Today I am walking a stretch of the Southern Upland Way, the national coast-to-coast path across Scotland. I am walking east to west, from Polbae to Balmurrie in Wigtownshire – and I am cheating because I took my car to the very end of the track above the Bladenoch valley and someone is going to meet me at the Dranigower Bridge on the Cross Water of Luce nine miles away, and then drive me over sixteen road miles back to collect my car. Without this most unnatural form of support I would have to walk more than twice as far to get from one welcoming habitation to another. The Southern Upland Way crosses some extraordinarily beautiful and wild country. However, there are two serious criticisms of it as a walker's route: some of the 'legs' are too long – up to twenty-seven miles, and no obvious way of breaking them up because there are no houses, no villages, not even many roads; *and* there is too much forestry, especially at the western end. Or, put another way, the problems of the Southern Upland Way are that it is simultaneously too 'wild' *and* too 'cultivated'.

It is early spring, a day of soft shimmering sunshine and a stiff breeze. The air is clean and sharp. The more easterly end of the walk has been clear-felled quite recently, opening up wide views, and from the top of Craig Airie Fell the emptiness stretches away northwards over the little Loch Derry onto the moor, eastwards towards the Galloway hills sharply profiled against the morning sky and southwards to the sea. Soon though the forestry closes in. The larch trees still look dark pink from a distance, but closer up their first tufts of needles are a green more vivid even than early beech leaves. It is a little eerie because the mosses, luxuriant from the long soaking of winter, are glowing somehow luminous in the sunlight. The path is rough and in places very wet. I see my first frogspawn of the year in what is no more than a puddle, and they will be dried out before they hatch. The curlews have recently come up from wintering on the Solway merses. My gold tan terrier runs among the trees, vibrantly coloured on the moss and well-camouflaged in the bracken and dead grass. It is a lovely day and I am a long way from anywhere. Throughout the whole walk I see no one else. The nearest farms, High Eldrig to the South and Miltonise to West are both over two more or less unwalkable miles away across extremely rough terrain – high peat moor, boggy and unkempt. At the back end of last year I was dive-bombed by a short-eared owl on the Loden Moss just outwith this forestry plantation. Already today I have seen roe deer and put up a hare, still half-white for the winter but with a band of brown along its back. I am alone in one of the empty places; out in the huge nothing.

Eventually I arrive at Laggangairn.

And I am not alone at all. I am accompanied, haunted here by layers of evidence, by at least five thousand years of human activity, creative and commercial, that has laid down at least eight different slices of sediment. Laggangairn is a place of exposed cultural strata.

Unexpectedly, the trees take a step backwards leaving an open area, and the path goes straight across it and past two huge vertical slabs of granite, each taller than me and quite close together: they are the Laggangairn standing stones.

They are very ancient, the Laggangairn stones. Archaeologists date them to the third millennium BCE. Once upon a time, long, long ago, for reasons that are more or less unimaginable and by methods that are baffling, some people that we know very little about, though from whom many of us are certainly descended, thought it was a good idea to create huge public works in what seem now to be distinctly peculiar places.

Like all Bronze Age stoneworks there is something mysterious, fey even, about the Laggangairn stones. I know they will be there when I come through the forest, yet every time there is something shocking in their presence, both unexpected and inevitable. They are of local granite, faced, smooth on both sides though irregular in outline. They stand there, lichen-coated yellow and grey above the new grass and unmoved, immovable. They were there before I was. They will be there when I have gone.

There are only two stones now, but once there was a full circle of them – fourteen probably. This cannot have been a casual enterprise, it was planned and organised and must have taken years to construct. One by one these huge stones, needing gangs of people to move, were brought here, faced, provided with deep secure pits and levered up to the vertical. So much hard work, so much time taken from the business of staying alive. It is marginal up here: over in the next valley where I live, even with quad bikes and single farm subsidy the hill farmers struggle. They work so hard and in such unfavourable weather and with a mean, acid and treacherously wet soil. They do not take time out to build cathedrals by hand. Stone circles have no obvious usefulness – they are not like hut circles or field systems or even chambered cairns where the dead can sleep. They are works of the imagination – they are art or ritual or both and they were constructed collectively. I do not know why. No one knows why.

We do know, though, that there was a complex if mysterious cultural life here. All over these apparently inhospitable moors there are the shadows and remains of field systems and hut circles and burned mounds and stone works and cairns and kilns. Less than fifteen miles away down on the coast there is *another* stone circle at Torhouse. They did not just do it once and then rest on their laurels. All that labour all over again and within walking distance ... And we know too that it is precisely the empty austere wildness of the place that has preserved the evidence of this culture. The moor is so unyielding and ungenerous that over the five millennia it was never 'improved', cleared for cultivation, brought under control. The wild has preserved and protected the cultural.

It happens all the time. Coppicing and pollarding are one of the signs of genuine ancient woodland. Human use and management preserved rather than destroyed such woods, and indeed lengthened the life of individual trees. Moreover, coppicing increases biodiversity. The relationship between the wild and the human is never one-sided.

Now, in the sunshine, I am leaning against one of the stones, feeling its roughness and solidness against my shoulders. At Laggangairn the stones are not fenced in or hedged about. So few people come here that they do not need to be kept away. This is a nice thought, until I notice that the stones are graffitied – scored or carved deeply – again, not casually but carefully and laboriously.

These are not 'Kilroy was here' (though perhaps he was) or 'Suzy 4 Bob' (though perhaps she is and they dallied here one long summer afternoon). The graffiti on the Laggangairn stones are the residual evidence of another, very different, cultural strata. What are carved here are crosses: crosses in various sizes. They are, of course, not as old as the stone circle, but they are surprisingly old. These are eighth-century crosses. They are carved here because Laggangairn was a major stopping point on the pilgrimage route to the shrine of St Ninian at Whithorn. Ninian is not quite as mysterious as those Bronze Age builders, but he is still mysterious. Sometime before 400 CE, before the Romans finally left Britain and nearly two centuries before Columba famously rowed his coracle over from Ireland, settled on Iona and 'converted Scotland', Ninian built the first Christian Church in Scotland, his *Candida Casa,* the White House. An almost exact contemporary of Augustine, legend says that he was trained by St. Martin of Tours in France. Despite the isolation of western Galloway and the real perils of travel, soon after his death in about 430 CE Whithorn was attracting pilgrims. In the seventh century Bede wrote about Ninian and the pilgrimages to Whithorn. For a thousand years, until the Reformation put an end to such adventures of the spirit, people came in boats from Ireland and Cumbria and on foot, along established routes to Whithorn. The pilgrims walked a long way – there is a known pilgrimage route from Tain, north of Inverness, right across Scotland – and a very rough way. They came down the Dee valley slightly to the west of Carsphairn – their needs sustained the *ferme-toun* at Polmaddy longer than most such communities survived, and then followed a route similar to the one that the Southern Upland Way now takes across the foot of Rhinns of Kells and the Range of the Awful Hand to Glen Trool, and then across the Cree and up onto the moors. Perhaps they made the road for themselves or followed some older trade route or drove road. Laggangairn made a meeting and resting place before final descent down the Luce valley, to the Machars and the shrine. After the twelfth century, when the Cistercian monks established themselves at Glenluce Abbey, Laggaingairn probably became less important, but still in a steady stream, enough of them to require specific laws in a lawless land, because there is a statute from 1427 controlling and directing their journey and their behaviour.

About half a mile east of Laggangairn and just off the Southern Upland Way are The Wells of Rees. They tend to get lost in bracken in the summer, but today if I had diverted from my route I could have found them easily enough – three drystone domes covering rather scanty seeping springs. They are mediaeval and were built and maintained by the monks from Glen Luce for the benefit of the leper colony located 'slightly to the North'. There are no signs of this now, but the wells are there, and the pilgrims must surely have some relationship to the decision to keep the poor lepers there rather than somewhere else.

They are gone now, the pilgrims and the monks and the lepers, leaving the silent crosses carved into the standing stones on what was then the naked hillside, and three little domes of stone half-lost in a wood. They passed lightly through this wild place, although presumably their presence helped sustain the farms and communities along the way. And in their turn they must have linked Galloway to the rest of Scotland. But it is a thin layer of sediment for a thousand years of cultural activity.

It happens all the time. Deep under our feet the tectonic plates crawl along the magma layer, moving at about the speed a fingernail grows. The Sinai desert replaces the low warm sea that was there before; the Indian subcontinent breaks loose like an iceberg from Gondwana, wanders northwards, and when it crunches into Laurasia it pushes up the Himalayas; the ice rolls down from the north and flattens the mountains into hills and then retreats leaving peat bog behind it. On the surface this barely shows. We would not guess any of it just from looking. Similarly, the pilgrims tramp across the moors for a millennium; they carve crosses, avoid lepers, depend on the hospitality of farms and monasteries and leave so little behind them that I can walk pretending I am in the wilderness. The relationship between the wild and the human is never one-sided.

I leave the standing stones eventually and plunge back onto the path through the forestry. It is extremely wet here and haggy; for a brief moment, as my socks are soaked above my ankles with dank squidgy mud, I want the Council, or the Forestry Commission or Scottish Natural Heritage or whoever's responsibility it is to come at once and improve the track. I only want my wildness *reasonably* wild. But my attention is diverted within a hundred metres by the ruin of a drystone wall.

It wriggles its way, a series of mossed hummocks and lichened granite, through the trees, stops abruptly where it crosses the path, and starts again on the other side. I am reminded sharply that whoever it was did in fact take laborious steps to improve the path.

Drystone walls are called dykes in Galloway. They are everywhere, miles out on hill or moor there they are running up steep slopes, leaping over burns and drainage ditches on now tottering arches, curving their way round the outcrops of extruding granite that mark the terrain so distinctly, stopping and starting randomly on open hillside, stumbled upon in dense bracken and Sitka spruce plantation. They are so prevalent here, as in other parts of the north, that they seem natural. They look as ancient as the standing stones and feel like part of the wild. But they are not – or not in the way they first seem to be. These walls created the wild, and not in a kindly spirit. To build them, to mark ownership and get in higher agricultural yields and rents, the land was 'cleared'. Cleared this time not of trees or scrub or rocks like the 'greened fields' in the valleys, but of people. The Highland Clearances are infamous, rightly, but the same process happened throughout the whole country. The enclosures of common land that drove poor John Clare mad in Northamptonshire, that peopled the colonies and created the Empire, went on remorselessly through the eighteenth and nineteenth centuries. The Lowland Clearances are forgotten, but the process was as ruthless and efficient here as in the Highlands and, interestingly, met with more organised resistance. Groups of agricultural workers of various kinds banded together, called themselves 'Levellers' – partly in memory of the seventeenth-century political radicals, and partly because their main action was levelling the new dykes – breaking them up and reopening enclosed land. The landlords called in troops to subdue them.

The walls were built, the farms made larger, supporting a

far smaller population, and people left. It did not work: neither the available capital nor the available fertility were sufficient. Away from the coastal plain, the rich land along the Solway, the margins for the new non-subsistence farming were too narrow. The depopulation has continued. Unworked, the land gave up, 'went back', as they say; the laboriously dug drainage systems collapsed and the peat and bog moved in. All this wild beauty I live in and love was created at the expense of people's livelihoods – a whole way of life destroyed wantonly. The walls created what we think of as the natural wild scenery of much of upland Britain.

They are beautiful, the ruined walls, but the building of them was cruel in another way too. Until quite recently the measure of walls and drainage that a tenant farmer had to build and maintain each year was specified in the lease. Most of the stones had to be carried from the small quarry that existed on almost all the farms up to wherever the wall was to be. More than six miles sometimes, and over terrain so rough that vehicles were useless – it was carried by two men, in something euphemistically called 'a wheel-less barrow': a trug with shafts that went over each man's shoulders. I look at those miles of wall out on the moor and I hate the years of pointless labour, damaged backs and lonely nights. The silence I love does not come cheap.

It happens all the time. A forest falls down, a layer of sediment flows over it and lithifies, crushing the organic matter so tightly that it lithifies too – now you have a coal seam. People dig out the coal, abandon the mine; the land slips, pioneer plants whose previous habitats have been claimed by more demanding flora take over the slag heaps and make a new wild place. There are wild places and human cultures tame them. But the reverse is just as true. There are cultivated places and the wild moves in. Usually it happens because of unconsidered consequences of human actions: you dam a river and create a desert; you put in a road and cowslips flourish on the verges because there are no ruminants alongside motorways. The walls are meant to tame and manage the wildness but they create a new desolation. The relationship between the wild and the human is never one-sided.

And here indeed, less than a minute's walk later, is a ruined steading. It is Laggangairn, after which – although they were here first – the standing stones are named. It stands in a larger clearing and there are quite extensive ruins: the house, with one gable wall still standing and the fireplace and entrance clearly visible. It looks out down a hill between the trees at a long view. For miles there are no other buildings visible. Above it are various piles of stones in various degrees of decrepitude – a barn, a walled enclosure of some sort, and some heaps of stone I do not have the skills to interpret, but which speak even to my ignorance of farming and life and energy. The whole sloping site is still drained off – it is less muddy here than in the forestry and a burn flows tidily down one side. There is a marshy area, almost but not quite a pond at the bottom of the hill. Oddly enough, I have found it more difficult to find out much about Laggangairn than about the Standing Stones or the pilgrimages. I am sure the information is there (the censuses for example), but I have so far failed to retrieve it. In 1888 a report from the Earl of Stair – the great landowner in these parts – describes the stones as 'far from any human habitation,' but the ruins do not look as though they were abandoned as much as a hundred and twenty-five years ago. I have found one story, without a date. The farmer at Laggangairn took a third still-vertical stone from the circle to make a lintel for a doorway. But immediately he brought it into the steading his dog went mad and bit him. He in his turn went crazy and died and his wife buried him under the stone he had stolen. This hardly sounds likely: what doorway would require so massive a lintel? How did he move it single-handed? Where is the grave? This is a story about living in rural isolation, though it was probably less isolated then.

The moors, like the Western Isles, are littered with deserted steadings. My own house was abandoned comparatively recently, only about fifty years ago, and was going back into ruin by the time I found it. Within less than an hour's walk I can see at least six ruined farms in various stages of decay – and the old maps assure me there were many more. There is no sign at all of Glenkitten – once my next-door neighbour. Looking at the OS map it is clear that there were several farms both above and below Laggangairn. But even so, even when there were more active farms and larger families, Laggangairn must have been a lonely place to live once the pilgrims were gone. The nearest village is New Luce, a mere six miles away, but it was not founded until the 1820s. Now Laggangairn is sheltered by the forestry plantations all around it; they hem the place in except for the long but narrow view southwards, but they also shelter it from the huge wild sweep of the high moors. In some senses it is easier to see Laggangairn as part of the wildness itself rather than a brave defeated attempt to manage or use it.

There is another sense in which Laggangairn and the other derelict steadings are part of the wild. When human beings give up the long struggle to manage the wild in places like this they leave behind them a new habitat – better drained than the surrounding area, better dug, better manured, with new kinds of surfaces and different sorts of protection. Nettles (which were introduced deliberately by the Romans) famously flourish where humans have lived; nettles invite new insects, the insects welcome birds that would otherwise reject a particular environment. And they are not alone. The past presence of cultivation increases biodiversity. This continues even now. The ubiquitous London Pride is so called because it quickly found a new niche in the blitzed ruins of cities. Even corrugated asbestos – because of its high pH – offers a new home to a whole range of mosses otherwise only found on natural limestone. My ignorance extends here too – I cannot look down the slope at Laggangairn or poke about in the fallen stones and know which flora and fauna are here only because of the long lonely slog of farming in this austere landscape and the ultimate defeat of that courageous enterprise. But I do know that it is so, and if I could read it as a palaeontologist reads the rock strata I would find the living fossils in the sediment laid down here.

It happens all the time. Sometimes in older woodland you will see a large black beetle with a startling and beautiful iridescent purple, violet, indigo underside: it is a dung beetle and its presence reveals that this particular wood was once pasture wood. Dung beetles need cattle grazing and therefore producing dung, which the beetles can carry underground to fertilise the woodland floor, allowing more cattle to graze there. (Luckily, since woods are no longer grazed, dung beetles can make do with deer dung if there is enough of it – but cow dung is what they like best.) Barn owls, for me one of the iconic fauna of wild places, are flourishing in Galloway precisely because there are so many ruined steadings; they are not called barn owls for no reason. They are flourishing too because helpful humans have 'improved' the disused barns from the owls' point of view by inserting owl boxes. House martins are declining in Britain because humans now keep their houses too well – house martins need houses, but houses with nooks and cracks and rough edges to attach their nests to. Urban foxes sneak into town along disused railway tracks and rejoice in a fast food culture. The relationship between the wild and the human is never one-sided.

The most obvious top sedimentary layer of human activity here is the forestry. From the very start of today's walk, until just before the Standing Stones, I have been on Forestry Commission land. Just East of Laggangairn the Commission's forest ended and I am now in the privately owned Purgatory Wood. (It is called the Purgatory Wood because it stands astride the Purgatory Burn, and they say that is so named because the monks from Glen Luce herded the lepers across it on their journey to the colony and it marked the point that they might never cross again. Like rocks, these sedimentary layers get mixed and confused, breaking through and mingling with each other.) In fact though there is no difference: the boundary is marked on the maps but not on the ground. Both were planted at much the same time, in the early 1970s, and both are continuous monocultures, mainly of Sitka spruce punctuated by stands of larch. Most plantation larch are hybrids of indigenous and Japanese larches; Sitka spruce is entirely an import.

The extent of post-Second World War commercial forestation in Galloway is mind-boggling – three hundred square miles of it. When Richard Hannay slipped off the train and took to the hills in *The Thirty Nine Steps* (1915) he walked broadly speaking northwards for several days and never saw a tree. Throughout his wandering he was constantly exposed to the view of a small aeroplane and could find no cover. Now the ex-railway line he was travelling on goes through the Galloway forest and his route would not have taken him out of it. The Purgatory Wood is at the very western end of this vast industrial complex. Galloway came late to the post-war forestry boom, but now it is ubiquitous and pervasive and has entirely changed the appearance of the whole region. And not just the appearance: the Purgatory Wood ends a mile or so north of where I live, and local people say that it, together with Arecleoch to the North and West of here, has changed the drainage of the whole valley, causing far faster rising and falling water levels and affecting farming, wildlife – especially the birds – and the ancient delicate plumbing systems of the steadings. It really is a new stratum, thick and widespread, laid down on the older landmass.

It is easy to hate the forestry. By and large I do. It was a sort of madness: the economic sums never added up, the environmental costs were never properly assessed, and the grants and tax incentives handed out gave little or nothing to the people whose ways of life were damaged. By the time these late plantations were put in all this was, or could have been, known; the need for pit-props and railway sleepers (the justification for the whole process between the wars) has disappeared; it was proven that forestry does not provide the employment that had been anticipated and the ecological concerns were surfacing. It feels like the last Ice Age – the forests, like the ice, just rolled in, flattening the landscape, killing species and reducing biodiversity. It is easy not just to hate the results, but to feel furious with the individuals behind the process

In fact, of course, plantation woodlands and forests are nearly as ancient as any other form of agriculture – there is a suggestion that their enthusiasm for hazelnuts may have led Bronze Age Britons into cultivating or at least managing hazel trees. By about 1800 the area of plantation woods in Scotland had overtaken that of ancient woods, and by 1870 this was the case throughout Britain (except in Essex and Cambridgeshire where it is not true yet). It is not plantation *per se* that is the problem – it is monoculture, and, in combination with that, large areas in which all the trees are the same age as well as the same species.

But it is healthy to remember that these trees will not be here forever. If you read a description of the Southern Upland Way that is more than three years old you will form a very different impression from the one I am trying to give here. The open views of the earlier half of the walk were not there: the eastern end of this Forestry Commission patch has been clear-felled;

the forest – in the sense of lots of trees planted close together – has gone, and now efforts are underway to regenerate it in a more sustainable and sympathetic manner. Clear-felling looks very ugly at first, and especially the clear-felling of coniferous trees because they do not regenerate on their old roots as most broad-leaf trees do. But give it time – and time supported by a whole new way of thinking which looks to encouraging and developing regeneration.

The Forestry Commission plans to clear-fell its trees at the Laggangairn end of the forest in 2011 and 2012. It seems likely, as they went in at the same time, that the Purgatory Wood trees will come down about then too. I am trying therefore to enjoy it while I can, without denying the relief I will feel when it goes. The biggest joys for me in this mood are the absence of any livestock, which makes walking with a dog infinitely less stressful; the utter loveliness of larch trees at this time of year as the massed branches move from pink to vivid fresh green and this contrasts so movingly with the red-orange leaf (or rather needle) mould on the ground; the extraordinary, and sometimes even spooky, silence of these forests – the aloneness and secrecy of them; and the startling pleasures of the breaks, of coming out of the forest and into the Laggangairn clearing, of never seeing the standing stones until they are very close up – the surprises in monoculture plantations are particularly delightful because I expect no surprises.

And already the next sedimentary layer is moving in. I have cheated a little in this narrative, by omission at least. Beside the standing stones, still neat and new, with metal legs and a glass cover, sloped for convenient reading, there is an 'interpretation board' with an historical account and an illustrated reconstruction, to help me see better what I am seeing. And in the middle of what was once the farmyard, between the ruined home and the remains of the barn, is the

Beehive Bothy. It is a simple and elegant contemporary design, and does indeed look very like an old-fashioned beehive with a domed roof; it is dry inside and always open. Walkers can sleep here on the wooden benches raised above the floor if they want to. It is free and there is no need to book. There is a visitors' book that informs me that on average two or three people pass through each day (or at least two or three who have pens and are not hiding from the law or otherwise unwilling to admit they were here) – although I have never seen any of them. The bothy sits lightly on the land. But it and the interpretation board and the way-markers and indeed the path itself are new silt, the new sedimentary material, which marks a new layer in the long symbiotic relationship between the wild and the human.

When the clear-felling happens around Laggangairn it will bring two further strata into view.

One is old. Galloway was the centre of the 'killing times': the persecution of the Covenanters – a hideously strict and undeniably brave group of religious and political fundamentalists. They were savagely intolerant themselves, and some of them wanted to establish a theocracy. They swore fidelity to 'the solemn League and Covenant' and found themselves at odds with the government of the seventeenth century. When their churches were closed, they met in the deepest wild hills for illegal 'conventicles'. They were hounded and sometimes shot. Up the Luce Valley and around Barrhill the landscape is littered with 'martyrs' graves,' many of them renewed and embellished in the nineteenth century when the Covenanters gained a romantic glamour. When the trees are gone, from Laggangairn I will be able to see the sharp rocky hump of Craigmoddie Fell where Alexander Linn was shot and buried in 1685, and where, within a little wall, his grave and several tablets still commemorate his obstinate, unlovable courage.

The other is new. The wind farm on Artfield Fell will be in

full view. At present it is rather a small wind farm, but it is about to grow. There will be a huge expansion of wind generation over this whole area. Even with the planning map I cannot quite work out which turbines I will be able to see from Laggangairn besides Artfield, but certainly a good number – at Arecleoch, Chirmorrie and Darnarroch. Their construction is already improving our roads and providing access to difficult wild places. I approve of wind farms and also find them beautiful – indeed, I do not really understand people who object to wind farms when they have tolerated forestry plantations and power pylons quite happily for so long. But wind farms need wild high places where the wind blows hard and free, and they will be one more element in the 'modernity stratum' of this area's human sediment.

It happens all the time.
The Standing Stones.
The Pilgrims' route.
The steading.
The Covenanter's Grave.
The walls.
The forestry.
The Southern Upland Way.
The wind farms.

Me. It happens with me. I walk here. I live here because I love the wildness of the high moors. I walk and live as lightly as I can, but even to think of 'walking lightly' is a human, cultural thing. My desire both undermines wildness and supports its continuation. The relationship between the wild and the human is never one-sided.

Beached Wales

Susan Richardson

It's 1996.

You're in the passenger seat of a mini-bus, winding through a rain-thrashed landscape which would be feeling increasingly quiet and remote were it not for the American summer school students yapping away in the seats behind. You're in the midst of teaching a Travel Writing course and you're taking your students on a field trip, to the place they have to write about for their next assignment. You crane your neck, hoping for a glimpse of the sea through the windscreen wipers' strokes, but manage to spot only a clump of gorse, a few battered rocks and a sheep that looks like all the life has been flattened out of it by the weight of cloud and rain. Even if it were the most stunning of summer days, however, you'd find it hard to appreciate the view because you really don't want to be here. You want to be travel-writing yourself, not teaching others to do so. You want to be in some exotic, far-flung destination: anywhere but in Wales.

The bus passes a weathered footpath sign, stutters over some stones and comes to a sudden stop where the road runs out. You push open the door, clamber down from your seat and struggle, in the wind, to zip up your waterproof. Your gaggle of students straggles along behind as you walk the short distance from the bus to the brink of a precipitous cliff which overlooks a huge expanse of sand and the gruel-grey sea.

'Omigod...'

'It's, like, wow...'

'...awesome.'

The wind snatches all these platitudes and flings them over the cliff. Your students go through the usual photo-taking ritual, manufacturing smiles for the benefit of the camera, then huddle together, shivering.

'How about taking the footpath down to the beach?' you suggest. 'Remember, you've got to write an assignment inspired by what you see today, so it's important that you try to get a feel for the place and make lots of notes.'

They look down at the distant beach, then up at the relentlessly black sky and pull faces at each other. Awesome though they claim this place to be, you realise that any notes they're going to make will be from the seats back on the bus.

Feeling a mix of irritation at their lack of spirit and relief that you have some time to yourself, you stay standing in the rain on the edge of the cliff. To your surprise, you can just about make out a group of surfers, sleek as seals, launching themselves into the waves far below. Surfing isn't something that you've ever associated with this part of the world. Even though you were born and raised in Wales, you've spent much of the past decade elsewhere, most recently in surf-savvy Australia, and you've obviously lost touch with what's going on here.

The rain gets heavier, propelling you away from the cliff edge. Your mind lingers longingly on your sun-soaked Australian life, as you trudge up the lane away from the bus, in search of some shelter. The only rain-free zone is a little stone church – as you drip your way inside and take off your hood, your eyes fall on a cream-coloured plaque on one of the walls. 'In memory of Edgar Evans, a native of this parish,' it says, 'who perished on the 17th February 1912 when returning from the South Pole.' You remember learning about this ill-fated Antarctic expedition, led by Captain Scott, when you were at school, and though you recall that Evans died from a mixture of starvation, injury and exhaustion, you never realised that he was born here in Rhossili, on the westernmost tip of the Gower Peninsula.

You perch on a pew and ponder on the epic distance

he travelled from South Wales to the South Pole. Would he have come back to the place of his birth, you wonder, had he survived? Or would he have joined another expedition and moved on again?

What would have been a strong enough reason to make him stay?

It's 1998.

You're hauling yourself up to the top of the sandstone ridge which forms the backdrop to the three-mile stretch of beach below. You pass gorse bushes bursting with yellow flowers and two nuzzling brown ponies. In spite of these signs of spring, however, there are snowflakes in the air and your breath makes mist like ghostly bubblegum as you pant your way higher.

Slogging up the slope a few steps ahead of you is a man who was born in Bavaria to German parents, who moved to Cardiff as a child and who claims, proudly and unhesitatingly, that he's Welsh. On this, the first full day you've spent with him, he's invited you to don your walking boots and accompany him to one of his favourite wild Welsh places.

He has also, you discover, when you eventually make it to the trig point marking the highest spot of the ridge, brought his favourite food for a picnic. Olives. Artichoke hearts in herbs and oil. Crusty bread. Goat's cheese. You pull your woolly hat down over your ears, zip up your fleece as high as it will go and sit on a rock, half-facing him and half-facing the view. You can't see any surfers in the sea today but there's a flock of hang-gliders leaping from the ridge a few hundred metres from your picnic place, all of them willing, it seems, to trust both the updrafts of air and their own nerve to keep them airborne.

As you munch on a hunk of bread and cheese, you reflect that today, apart from the conviction of the hang-gliders, everything about the scene seems vague and indecisive. Spring hasn't quite made its mind up – though the gorse is blooming, its flowers are getting sprinkled with snow. The craggy promontory jutting up out of the water at the southern tip of the bay hasn't quite committed to becoming an island, while however hard you stare at the boundary between the sea and the sand way below, you can't tell if the tide's in ebb or in flow.

'Hope you like chocolate.'

You pull your gaze away from the view and frown at him. 'Sorry?'

'Chocolate. I hope you like it.'

Your frown morphs into a smile. 'Doesn't everyone?'

He hands you a small gift box. Inside is a clutch of chocolate Easter eggs resting on a bed of shredded brown paper to make it look like a nest. You take one, peel back the gold wrapping and bite. The flavour floods your mouth like summer.

You'd like to stay and share the other eggs but it's too cold to sit any longer and he's started to pack away the remains of the picnic into his rucksack. From his earlier description of the walk, you know you'll soon be following the ridge past the scattered stones and cairns of ancient burial grounds, then dropping sharply down to the sand dunes at the northern end of the beach for the return stretch back to Rhossili.

Sand dunes. Something else that's shifting and indecisive.

You sigh and make to lever yourself up off the rock.

He stretches out his hand to help you.

'Ready?'

It's the year 2000.

Today is the last day-trip, in a long history of day-trips, which you will share with your mother, but neither of you knows this yet. As a child, you were taken on outings to Somerset and Devon: even though you were born in the Welsh border county of Monmouthshire, your mother always insisted you were English, so you never ventured further west into Wales for any family holidays. This time, however, you're the one who's chosen the destination and made the day-trip possible. You want your mother to see what you consider to be the most magnificent stretch of coast in the whole of Britain, if not the world. You want to show her how much more inspiring it is here in Rhossili than in crowded resorts like Weston-super-Mare and Torquay.

You help your mother from the car and wait as she tries to ease out her stiff legs. She declines to use her walking stick, preferring to hook her swollen hand through your arm instead. On the end of your other arm, clipped to a lead, is your mother's terrier, Benjy. He pulls you both towards the cliff edge, intent on investigating every blade of grass, every rock, every sheep dropping en route.

The three of you make your way to a bench with a gull's-eye view of the beach. It's mid-June and an idyllic summer's day. The sea is tropical-turquoise, the sand Daz-white, and there's barely the hint of a breeze.

You point out the ridge along which you and your partner always walk, the sand dunes piled up like happy memories, the tidal promontory where you secretly want to get stranded as the poet Dylan Thomas once did. You explain to your mother that the name of the promontory, Worm's Head, probably comes from the Anglo-Saxon word 'wurm', meaning 'serpent', which aptly describes the shape of the land slithering up out of the water, although the full extent of its body, a rocky causeway, is only visible a few hours either side of low tide. Your mother listens carefully and nods, asks if the coast of Devon can be seen from here, though not in a wistful way.

Benjy, meanwhile, is much less enchanted by the view than you are. His nose is glued to the ground and he's tugging on his lead, impatient to move on.

'Why don't you take Benjy down onto the beach, love?'

'He'll be fine up here,' you say, untangling his lead from the bench leg. 'He'll soon settle.'

'I don't mind the two of you leaving me for a bit. Go and enjoy yourselves.'

'I'm enjoying myself here, Mum. And I don't want to leave you on your own.'

'Look at him pulling – he needs a good run.'

You watch him sniff the air, ears pricked, as itchy for further exploration as you yourself used to be, and you smile.

Your mother's face crinkles into a smile too. 'I'll be happy as Larry here, honest I will. It's lovely.'

With Benjy leading the way, you head down the steep, stepped footpath from the cliff top, wishing your mother were fit enough to see how extraordinarily lovely it is at beach-level too. Will the new treatment she'll soon be starting improve her mobility, you wonder? Or will she become increasingly disabled, with the space she inhabits becoming ever-more confined?

Benjy leaps down from the last step onto the beach and races towards the ribs of the wrecked ship, the *Helvetia,* which are sticking up out of the sand. He methodically lifts his leg against each one, then scampers on, stub-tail wagging, a black scribble on an otherwise gloriously empty white page.

Instead of running after him, you turn, look up at the cliff and wave at the place where you know your mother to be.

Humber

Katharine Macrae

If you look at it on the map Spurn Point appears as a bent hairpin, slightly to the right of Hull, curving out into the North Sea and then back on itself. What it is, is a thin spit of land, of sand, of shingle, that separates the wide and terrifying mouth of the Humber from the equally terrifying North Sea. Towards the tip there is a lighthouse, which has fallen into disuse because the spit, every quarter of a millennium, breaches and the whole thing starts again. Beyond that, a lifeboat station, likewise awaiting abandonment. Spurn is felt to be nearing the end of this particular incarnation. And although there is a road along it, the road is made of flat square tiles as the spit, sinuous as a cat, shifts constantly under it, and the road has to be remade, rearranged, in a new place, wherever the spine of the land finds rest.

It is a hot night in early July and I have just kissed my daughter goodnight. She is staying with my mother while I drive over to Hull, where an old friend is having a party. I don't seem to have any money, although I have always had a soft spot for luxury, and I cannot really justify two nights, alone, in a newly opened boutique hotel. It has occurred to me that if I were to spend the first night at Spurn Point, which would be free, and the second night in the new hotel, then I can combine my slightly wayward passion for the asperities of the North with the subsequent guaranteed comfort of crisp cotton sheets and Molton Brown bath products.

I still haven't really made up my mind to go at this hour but my mother, who is eighty, persuades me. I sit on the end of her bed, the two of us drinking tea. The car is packed; I could just as well drive over in the morning.

'If you go now,' she says, 'you'll be there for sunrise.'

And her pale eyes, blue as forget-me-nots, but softer, hold mine. Eighty. The bones of her hands are as frail yet pliant as feathers. This lovely lady, this impassioned wanderer, she wouldn't have hesitated for a moment. So I kiss her soft cheek, and laugh, and go out into the night, no need for a map, just head east, past Manchester, towards morning.

Crossing the central ridge of the Pennines feels exciting – the highest motorway in England, the journey surprisingly swift. But then the road passes along the north bank of the Humber for what seems to be the longest time. In Hull the docks spill on, kilometre after kilometre: I haven't looked at a map and I am beginning to regret it. Although I know where I'm going, to the place that separates the sea from the river. So if I follow the river, I'll get there. And yet – I hadn't thought it would be so far beyond Hull, so far beyond the city. A strange flat landscape opens up to the east, definite against the imperfect dark. Little villages, picturesque, sleepy, but then a triple-stretch white limousine parked, jaunty, by a village green. I pass a farmyard filled with gypsy caravans, where a little wooden windmill powers the perpetually nodding head of a clown-like wooden man – truly strange – beyond the world's end. A nuclear power station appears. Wind farms. The detritus of extremities. I am reminded of Dungeness, another limbo, where the filmmaker Derek Jarman lived out his last years in a black and yellow shiplap cottage, dragging an exquisite garden from the blue grey shingle as his once-keen eyes foundered, then failed. There is a photograph of him as a smiling Canute, wrapped in a regal cloak with a necklace made of fishing floats, pitching himself between the land and the sea, ordering back the waves. Or perhaps it is Lear, another fighter against the futility, or inevitability, of dying light. And yet, despite the echo, Dungeness seems curiously far away. Smaller, and harder. There is a softness about this landscape, a vastness to it, which I had not anticipated.

Eventually I reach the village of Easington, and the signs for Spurn Point itself. There is a car park, although to use it seems slightly unnecessary, but I do. It is alongside a campsite of park homes. I lock the car, go back, check it. Am irritated with myself for doing so. It is, after all, not yet two in the morning. Who would come here now? I walk through farmland, pass a number of houses. And am surprised how many lights are on. I really hadn't thought to be so close to other people, and thought those that were here would be sleeping.

I try to suppress a rising panic, an anxiety. I feel sure it's to do with this unexpectedly populated aspect of where I am, and the consequent vulnerability of walking alone onto this narrow strip of land. After all, there's no place to turn. It's like walking the plank. I had acknowledged the possibility of the odd bird-watcher, but at this time of year, and in a place so remote, had believed it unlikely. And yet now, behind pulled curtains, I feel eyes fixed on television sets, cans of lager warming in the summer night. Young mothers with sleepless children, shift workers, the very old. I sense their wakefulness.

Headlights approach, a police Range Rover. It pulls over – the occupants, dough-faced, currant-eyed – peer at me; I raise a cautious hand. What are they looking for? Smugglers? Suicides? Vice? They seem satisfied that I am none of these, though do not reciprocate my wave. They drive on, out towards the point.

Where the arm of sand first lifts out from the body of the land – so that both the river, and the sea, become visible – there is a collection of prefabricated dwellings, of corrugated iron and precast concrete. A number of cars, including an old BMW, are strewn, rather than parked, outside. One of the buildings, a Nissan hut, seems to have been a café serving visitors to the point, but the signs look old and abandoned. Yet the cars imply that someone lives here still, that there are other inhabitants of the fringe. My plan had been simply to walk out across the spit, to the tip, where the river meets the sea, and then lie down, and sleep. I had thought that I could spend the day here – tomorrow, that is – exploring, absorbing. But I hadn't fully comprehended how little darkness there would be. None, in fact, maybe a shadowing, a filling in, soon after midnight, but since then the sky has been gradually lightening, dark blue, now curiously streaked. It is easy to see the pale curves of sand ahead of me, like watching a movie in black and white, the colour slowly emerging, a Polaroid. The police pass by again. In just a few minutes they have completed the trip which I have driven through the night to undertake.

I walk over to the river mouth. Its shore is flat and fecund, green marsh, brown mud. There is a popping sound, as though a hundred mouths suck bull's-eyes. Marsh gas, I suppose. And the river itself. Vast. As wide and real as death. A few kilometres upstream a single-span suspension bridge joins Lincolnshire with the East Riding of Yorkshire; it's a popular place for suicides. I wonder how many of them float out this far, have washed up on this shore. I am afraid to look at the water, afraid of what I might see. A bloated dog, pale limbs like chairlegs pointing at a sightless sky.

Or worse.

My almost nauseous unease is accentuated by a sound – and one so distinctive, so defining of this place, that I feel sure I would know it if I were brought here blindfold. It is a deep vibration, a plainsong, a confluence of many voices. At first I think it is an accident formed by the air's architecture, where the river-wind meets the sea-wind. And this may yet be so, but in the paleness of the summer night I can see the instrument in which the notes are caught. The purflings, the bridges, are the electricity poles which run out to the lighthouse, and to the lifeboat station beyond. Any electrical current runs silent through these wires, or at any rate its gentle hum is suppressed below the song, which is ceaseless, low and continuous as madness.

I turn away, and walk over to the beach on the other side of the spit.

The more space I put between myself and the wakeful inhabitants of the mainland, the better I feel. The sea is beautiful, pearl grey, opaque, and the sky lightens constantly above it with a bloom as soft as a plum. Sunrise seems imminent but I know it's not for another hour or so. A rusted raffia and metal chair retrieved from the sea and set up on the sand attests to the presence of fishermen, or birdwatchers, but not now. I like being alone. I settle into my gait, happy that mine are the first footprints, in sand as new as snow.

Over the years there have been attempts to stop the spit from breaking, to protect it from the combination of long-shore drift and the river's passage that forms it, destroys it, and will form it again. These various schemes now present themselves as so many abandoned works. Ballast, in concrete blocks. The ribs of groins, each one made from a single tree, the bars of a giant cage along the shore. The horizontal planks have long since washed away, or been removed, as the futility of what they were attempting became apparent. Now, left, these upright posts have the gravitas of gods, each one as thick as a man, and twice as tall. I am reminded of Easter Island, the sightless heads that guard the land. The skeleton of a Viking ship, its king and cargo ash. I am delighted by this place, have forgotten about my fear, and am still running about between the forest of posts when the sun lifts out of the sea, orange into an indigo sky. I am surprised by the warmth as it lights my face. As though a stranger had reached out and touched me, in greeting, or reprimand. Shadows! I hadn't thought of that. Incredible long, thin, shadows. Suddenly, to the right of me, I see my own. Tall, and spectre-thin, my long hair blown sideways, my arms tiny above the endless scissor legs. And suddenly my face is wet, tears from nowhere, my shadow. My shadow. I stand between it and the sun, between it and the earth, and for this little time I know I am alive. This moment, these moments, of recognition. They come so rarely. The realisation of living now, without hindsight, without forethought, the time that passes even as we enter it.

I become accustomed to the day, relish the light wind, the turning tide, the water easing back. And now I can see everything, each beach-combed fragment, each piece of rope, of driftwood, old toy, bits of net, pram. Absolutely nothing unexpected. And then a ruin! A cottage, a bothy; without roof, or doors or windows, half-sunk into the sand. It must have been built on the spit, when the spit was somewhere else, and as the snakelike course shifted, this house, long abandoned, has ended up on the beach, disappearing under the water with each spring tide. I explore the little house, but I want to get on and it's tiring, walking on sand. I head up into the low dunes and am thrilled with what I find. Snap dragons and sea holly, convolvulus and sea pinks. Saxifrage, pink – everything pink. *Rosa rugosa* flourishes, but arches sideways like a bramble, presumably self-seeded from someone's garden; and then a star-shaped flower, yellow, my mother has it in her garden, another escapee made good. I am enchanted with the softness of the landscape.

I see the lighthouse. Something from a children's tale.

And I see him. The man.

At first I think he's fishing. He stands, or rather acts, halfway between me and the lighthouse. I can't be sure of his age; I don't want to get close enough to look. He could be anything between twenty-five and fifty. I realise he hasn't seen me, so I drop into the marram grass, aware suddenly how tired I am – I've been awake all night. He looks like Frank Auerbach, the painter, thick-set, thick hair, energetic, strong. And yet he runs at the sea like a dancer, stops – almost on tiptoe as his arms fly forward, and then hugs himself, runs back, but backwards, never once taking his eyes from the sea. He picks up a rock, runs again at the water's edge, hugs the rock to him, to his chest, and then hurls it, with all he's got. It is this movement, I now see, that I had mistaken for casting, for fishing. He's throwing. His arms fall, free of their burden, and he pauses to see where the stone has landed. Although it's in the water. But he is still only for a moment. He seems to rail at the sea, lifts his arms in despair, or supplication, then runs again, his strange dance. And he repeats it, another rock, hugged down to the water, thrown, watched, the same backward, erratic movement. Every so often he reaches the sea empty-handed, seemingly because he hasn't found an appropriate stone in the time he has allowed for each circuit, and that's when the arms fly outwards, followed by the hug.

I am curious, yet quite afraid of him. I try not to think about Virginia Woolf, and her book *To The Lighthouse,* and how they never got there until everyone was old, or dead, and it was too late. I have no desire to pass this man to reach my destination. And I am so very, very tired. The dunes are full of little indentations, clearings among the sea holly and marram grass, protected from the wind. Keeping one eye on the man, I move behind him in an arc. I see an old green car by the little road, this side of the lighthouse, and think it entirely possible that he has got here using it. The only footprints on the beach have been my own. I find a track leading from the road to the beach, between me and the car. There are absolutely no footprints in the dunes. So he's driven here, or walked, but either way he hasn't come over the ridge of dunes, or along the beach, which leaves the road, and the river bank, as the spit is only a few metres wide at this point. And he is certainly a creature of the most compulsive habit.

So I retreat back into the dunes, keeping more or less equidistant from the track, the beach and the road, and scoop a deeper hollow with my fingers in the warming sand, at the place furthest from where I feel he is likely to pass. I lie down in it, curl up, foetal. I cannot see anything but marram grass and sky. I am below the lip of the dune. I cannot see him. Which means, I suppose, that he cannot see me.

I close my eyes for the soft sand blows constantly; I find my mind returning to an event a few weeks earlier when I had met up with my husband in London. We were staying in an hotel and I woke early. I had walked over to the window and, while he slept, watched as the hard summer light picked the shadows from the mews street below, first drawing detail, brickwork, cobbles; then bleaching it, until everything glowed and hazed with the promise of heat. I watched a man come out of a house, as though to leave for work: he wore a suit, a flare of white indicating his shirt, too bright to see if he wore a tie. He had a cup in his hand, which surprised me. And then I realised: a smoker. I imagined a child in a high chair at a kitchen table, the mother or au pair in attendance. As he lit the cigarette, everything about him seemed to come together, his very atoms coalesced, formed a cloak about him, a little swirl of testosterone. I watched him relax into himself, become a man, and everything that is female in me rose up, attentive, curious.

Later, I walked past the house and saw that it wasn't a home but an engineering consultancy. This made more sense of his tension, his distraction, his abstraction, and also of his desire for the cigarette. When you want something, and you can't have it, there is a tension inherent in the situation. I wonder idly what has happened to the man on the beach, what has brought him to this place, this erratic dance, this compulsion. But I am unable to hold the thread. Sleep worries constantly at the fabric of my consciousness, loosening it, pulling at it before lifting it, so that it blows and dips over the sand like a child's favourite blanket, carrying all my wakeful thoughts away with it.

I wake up an hour or so later. The satiety that only sleep can give. Sand covers me in little drifts; my hair is full of it. Warm in my hollow basin, heavy lidded. I sit up. Cautious. I am incredibly hungry; I have food and water with me, but am already ill-at-ease, and will remain so until I know the whereabouts of my companion.

I walk to the tip of the dune, bending forward slightly to reduce my height, the lighthouse to my right, the beach to my left and ahead of me. And there he is, still throwing rocks. I catch now the 'O' of his voice, no words, the wind has shifted. It is as though nothing has happened (nothing has happened); perhaps he's a little slower, but not much. I wonder, for the first time, how long he's been here. Did we arrive more or less together? Or had he been here all the while that I drove, over the Pennines, along the estuary, under the deepening sky? But I don't really want to know, not now, possibly not ever. I want to be free of him, away. I am very much afraid of this man. I feel it coiling in my intestines.

My heart pulses at the base of my throat, my mouth is dry. I am still so tired; one hour's sleep is not so much and I am jittery with adrenaline. We are four kilometres into the North Sea, he and I, the murderous estuary to the west. At some point he is likely to leave – I had hoped this would happen while I slept, leaving me to follow him, leisurely, off the peninsula. But no, it will be he who follows me. I don't believe he came along the beach, but the sand is too slow, and tiring at best, exhausting now, to walk along. The road will be in full view of him. In spite of this I decide to remain visible – he seems settled for a while – and make distance. I reach the little road of tiles, and I run.

Because most of me suspects the man to be harmless, I

cannot find the necessary edge. My fight-or-flight mechanism is folded, resting, just below the surface, and I cannot access it. I am irritated that I am running away from this place that I have come so far to see. I simply cannot believe the literary irony of not getting to the lighthouse, which is wonderful, full-bodied with black and white hoops, like an Everton mint, its decommissioned light held in a black liquorice cage with diamond sugar panes. I know that if I was a man, and I was ten years younger, I wouldn't care; and am irritated that my blonde hair and slight frame render me vulnerable, unexpected. I wish I'd brought a hat. And yet it's not a big thing. Not really. I'm sure that most men ten years younger would be doing exactly what I'm doing now: namely, running away from a madman. If they'd even thought to come here in the first place.

A hare appears; huge, brown, with unmistakable black ears, the slightly devil eye. It seems so large that it fills the road. I stop. Quite unperturbed, it lopes off in the direction of the river. Had it come from the beach? What a thought. And I am happy, suddenly everything is all right. If I hadn't run away from the madman, I would never have met the hare. I follow it. The riverbank, which had previously seemed a place of terror, seems, under the warm sun, quite lovely. The light on the water renders it accessible; possibly this also is an effect of the receding tide. Even as I watch a great ship enters the river mouth, brightly coloured and flat as cardboard, bound for Hull and full of purpose. On the far bank, impossibly far away, is a town, rows of little towers and cubes, something made on a children's TV show from matchboxes and toilet rolls. Not Hades. Cleethorpes.

I walk along a little track through short bright grasses following the path of the hare. Every so often it reappears before me, in exactly the same aspect, facing west, towards the river. Its hazel eye seems to appraise me before it turns once again and lopes off, apparently as tame as a cat. Suddenly all around me are oystercatchers. I hear them before I see them and laugh out loud when I do. They float like an articulated carpet, like something from Aladdin, washing over the sand and onto the river bank, pouring through grass, across the track, opening to circumvent a stone, or a bit of wood, and closing around it on the other side, their shifting pattern hovering above a movement smooth as castors. And their funny chirruping sound, again like castors. Mechanical birds. I suppose they have gone to the river, because quite suddenly they are gone, and it's as though they were never there.

I can see a fisherman now, ahead of me. Broad-shouldered, yet slender, my eye is drawn by the suppleness of his back. I could avoid him, he hasn't seen me, but I am not afraid. I continue to walk along the path. Closer now. Around thirty, and unshaven, he is reeling in his line. He glances at me and nods. There is a smile implied in the gesture and humour in his expression, although this could just be an effect of the sunlight, his eyes half-closed against it. I return the greeting, inclining my head fractionally, aware of a Japanese quality to this silent exchange of nodding courtesies. I think of the Willow Pattern, the blue and white plates, although they were Chinese and the figure on the plate carries a whip. The fisherman looks at the tip of his rod and fiddles with it, the movement slightly exaggerated; I have probably surprised him. I know that he is checking the whereabouts of the hook, and that this is for my benefit. So I loop behind him in acknowledgement of this, allowing him room to cast. I walk on without looking back.

The hare has gone, the riverbank is not my demesne, so I make my way back up to the road, then back onto the beach, toward the mainland.

I am curiously disappointed as I walk back through the prefab buildings. It seems silly, now, to have been afraid, to have abandoned my journey. And yet. I walk back towards the car. Notice immediately that one tyre is low, and liquid seeps from underneath the engine. I reach down, touch the liquid; it's clear, no smell. Water. That's something then. I glance at the wheel on the front driver's side, examine the tyre. It's soft, but not too bad and there is no obvious damage to it. I listen, but there is nothing; no hiss of air. The little cap has been removed. So. Not a puncture. I open the door and reach for a bottle of water, it's surprisingly cold and misted with condensation. I flick the switch that releases the bonnet. With one hand I hold the bottle as I drink, long, slow, cool. With the other, I raise the bonnet. I flex my foot against the bumper, watching for the movement of the water in the radiator reservoir. It seems OK. I check the container that feeds the windscreen wipers. Tip the rest of my bottle into it.

A man appears. I hadn't heard him approach and there is no sign of a car but, at this point, nothing surprises me. He is about sixty, heavy-set, wearing baggy denim dungarees and a pair of Crocs. No socks, no shirt; indeed, he appears to be naked beneath the dungarees, the sides unbuttoned to reveal pale flesh, but he wears a navy blue and white bandana around his head, Hell's Angel-fashion. Presumably to hide his encroaching baldness, if the few wispy tufts that are visible are any indication of what is underneath. A large pair of binoculars hangs around his neck, gold sovereign rings gild the fingers that rest there. A twitcher.

'Someone's let your tyres down,' he offers, surprisingly well informed. 'And there's liquid coming out of your engine.' The pitch of his voice is light but nasal and this, in combination with his elongated Hull vowels, creates an incongruously effeminate effect in such a big man. I notice a large, hooped earring.

'I think it's from the air-conditioning,' I say.

He is standing in the long grass at the side of the car park, and seems unwilling to step onto the tarmac.

'That's good,' he says. 'Well. I can see that you're on your own, so I'll leave you in peace. Not disturb you.' And he sets off in the direction of the beach. I smile to myself, trying to work out what he'd have said if I'd had company, but am nonetheless touched by his gentle grace, and the implied understanding of what it is to be alone. I look around me. How many pairs of eyes? What a curious place. I get into the driver's seat. I am about to turn the key in the ignition when I see the hare again. Or rather, a hare. It is cropping grass on the bank ahead of me in more or less the place where the man had stood a few moments earlier. The word *psychopomp* forms in my mind. Meaning spirit guide.

I turn the key. The hare looks up at the sound, curious, deer-like, but unruffled. It goes back to pulling at the grass. I put the car into reverse, and leave.

I am able to fill the tyre at a service station on the outskirts of Hull. The people at the hotel are very kind; they let me check in early, and give me a breakfast of fish, fruit and coffee on the house while my room is being cleaned. It is still only nine o'clock. When the room is ready, instead of saying thank you, I make a fuss, would they mind awfully? But I really want a view. They are about to clean another room, then think better of it, and upgrade me to a suite. I get a view, am most thankful, then draw the curtains across it and slip between the predictably white sheets of an unnecessarily large bed.

The image of the madman returns to me. His ceaseless dance, his searching gaze, his hugged then rejected rocks. My memory spirals against my will, retrieving and assembling unwanted fragments, a different time, another place. It had been evening when I heard them return. The green parrots that are so common in that part of Barcelona were squabbling in the palm trees outside. I opened the door. As I lowered my hand a single thread of sticky liquid, dark as peat – and which in washing my hands

I had somehow missed – ran the length of my arm from elbow to wrist. It waited, viscous, at the base of my thumb and then fell, sticky, onto the tiled floor. All eyes followed it.

'Oh, I'm so sorry,' I said, because in watching this strange spectacle my callers had inadvertently been left out in the cold. 'Come in.' A new neighbour, with a little girl in my daughter's class, had very kindly offered to bring her home from school. My child's face was as white as chalk. I don't think her friend had noticed. 'Would you like some tea?'

'I'll do that,' said the kind neighbour, relieved, no doubt, to have something to do.

'Yes. I'll just go and wash my hands,' I said, to put everyone out of their misery. The peaty thread was now drying, tightening into tiny wrinkles, and as it did so I noticed, for the first time, the ox-blood half-moons under each nail and the powdered tracery of rust in the lines of my hands. My daughter followed me, shadowed me, her eyes wandering, fearful. My brave girl. I was numb. Quite numb.

Later, over the tea, I asked my neighbour if she would stay with me a while. Of course, of course. The children were playing. Oblivious. She has three children, she told me, a grown-up son and two younger ones, this last one born when she was forty-two. I had a sudden sense that she was, at that moment, embarrassed by her fertility.

'I've never had a miscarriage,' she offered.

'It's all right ... I have. It's just low blood pressure. I'll be fine. But it's nice to have someone around.' I excused myself. Politely. And quietly passed the first of what are referred to as the products of conception.

I had realised, when I woke that morning, that on this day I might lose the child that had died inside me three weeks earlier. I had spent the day with a girlfriend. After dropping our children at school we walked on the mountain at the back of Barcelona, trying to induce the contractions. Later her mother was waiting with an enormous stew: veal, peas and hard-boiled eggs. High in protein. High in iron. Familiar with suffering, and eminently practical, the older people of Barcelona call a spade a spade.

'You must drink a lot of water, and keep up with your salt.'

My fridge was full of isotonic drinks, enough to run a marathon. Enough to replace the fluid I would lose, without the indignity of going to the hospital. Many people had invited me to stay with them, offered to look after our daughter, offered to stay with me. My doctor had expressed her concern that I would not come to the hospital. Her secretary, when I called to cancel the anaesthetist, was more brutal:

'I understand your husband is in London. There'll be no one for you if you haemorrhage in the night.'

'No one where?' I asked. 'Do the emergency services no longer work 24/7?' I was sick of being interfered with. Bored with being polite. I wanted to be alone. And my daughter was afraid, did not want to go away, we have no family here.

Sometimes it's better to be at home.

The next morning the same good neighbour called to take my daughter to school. Later, some friends took me to a café in our local square. I was weak – I stumbled twice – but felt good. I sat beneath a plane tree, enjoying the warmth of the sun on my face, the shapes the leaves made through my closed eyelids. Caramelised coffee formed a memory in my mouth and I could feel it entering my blood in a thin tributary. I was restored by it. I heard the sounds of the women. My breasts were tender now the milk was coming in, and full; an aching pleasure just tipping towards pain. I looked around instinctively for the baby.

The baby.

The tricks our bodies play, and suddenly it rolled over me, all that work for nothing, and I was caught; unsure how to get through the hours until my little girl came back to me.

Routes

Ken Wilkie

I was born under a stone in the hills behind Dundee. That's what my mother told me when I was a little boy.

'Whereabout?' I asked, trying to visualize this.

'Oh, on the hillside,' she replied, nodding to the fields that sloped away northwards to the Sidlaw Hills. She sounded a little embarrassed.

'Did I come from under the ground?' I pursued.

'Enough of these questions,' she replied. 'Go out and play with the dog now.'

I did. But I couldn't let the revelation go.

When my father was home from one of his yearly trips to Scandinavia, he told me a bedtime story that in the northern Norwegian town of Hammerfest, winters were so cold that people covered the gravestones with sealskin coats. In my mind, stones were already a part of death, so why couldn't they also be a part of birth?

Lying awake, looking at the only image on my wall, an enigmatic black and white photograph of the midnight sun, I thought to myself: if there are graveyards, why couldn't there be birthyards?

I kept thinking about what my mother had told me. One morning, I didn't feel like playing in the garden or under the grand piano, which was the den I shared with the dog, from where I studied uncles' ankles and aunts' shoes as they pressed down on the pedals at weekend gatherings. Instead, I walked away from the house ... down Strathmartine Road, which narrowed as it passed through raspberry fields, across a stone bridge over the River Dichty, and up a hillside strewn with gorse bushes, birch trees and stones of all sizes.

Could this be the source of life, I wondered? Under these rocks, could I find a brother or a sister? Maybe even a friend.

As I lifted and tilted moss-covered stones off the ground, slaters scurried away and worms squirmed in the morning light. Unless my life had begun as a centipede, I wasn't having much success here. But I didn't give up. I lost track of time. And went on looking under stone after stone after stone after stone.

Meanwhile, back home, my mother was checking with the neighbours but no one had seen me, except Joe the cross-eyed grocer who had reported me heading north earlier that day. The police were alerted and a group of men were sent out to find the missing boy. I remember the search party approaching, dressed in tweeds but equipped, Dad's Army-style, with broom handles, cricket bats and sawn-off clothespoles.

'There he is!' yelled a man wearing a deerstalker who seemed to be leading the posse. They were glad to have found me all right. But I hadn't found what I was looking for.

My adult life as a journalist and travel writer has taken me many more times 'away from the house' since that first expedition. Looking for the source of the River Niger in Guinea, following Darwin in the Galapagos Islands, riding with Texas cowboys, trekking to a sacred valley in the Andes, diving on the coral reefs of Bonaire, digging for dinosaur bones in Colorado. From the frozen sea of Orkotsk in Japan to the steaming rain forests of Costa Rica, Panama, Surinam and Brazil, and from the world's slowest train in the Himalayas to the fastest magnet train in Shanghai, I have had as many misadventures as adventures. As Robert Louis Stevenson said, 'I travel not to go anywhere, but to go. I travel for travel's sake. The great affair is to move.'

I have often wondered what shaped my drive to explore the wilder parts of the world. For the first ten years of my life I could hardly have been described as adventuresome. I was a well-groomed city boy, an only child seen and not heard in a stern Victorian villa on the outskirts of Dundee, receiving a classical education at the High School, a prestigious grammar school founded in 1239 by the abbot and monks of Lindores. The school motto, *Prestante Domino* (Under the Guidance of God) had little to do with either nature or travel – with the exception of a gruelling journey for a twelve-year-old on a cattle boat *The Laird's Loch* from the Clyde across a rough Irish Sea to billet in a former POW camp at Magilligan.

Far from being at one with nature, I was shielded from it in a somewhat ironic way as a child. Instead of my father taking his Scandinavian business friends out for hikes in the hills to show them the beauty of Scotland, he took them on a grand tour of the Highlands in an old Rolls Royce. This meant that I was strapped into a kilt and appointed as a nine-year-old photographer with my Kodak fold-out camera. I had to sit all day in one of the fold-down seats that faced backwards, like London taxis. So my first observations with that camera produced black and white images of the ears and noses of Scandinavians, looking at odd angles at the mountains out of the car window. Viewed today, I suppose they were the equivalent in stills of video clips with pop stars cruising in the back of stretch limos.

But as I entered my teens, I began to cycle with friends to the Arbroath cliffs and explored the red sandstone caves that wormed far underground and were pounded into unpredictable forms by the North Sea. The cliffs and caves were sprayed with myth and unsolved mysteries. Courting the supernatural, I kept an ear open for the phantom piper who once disappeared there and whose lament is said to be heard moaning in the wind. I was encouraged to write about my adventures for the school magazine, but it was a series of stories in the boys' weekly magazine *The Eagle* about the adventures of a young reporter, and later the short stories of Dylan Thomas as a reporter in Wales, that sparked off my desire to be a journalist.

My life changed dramatically at this time with the death of my father. For months before his death I was not allowed to visit his bedroom. Nor did I attend his funeral. Following his death, my grandmother and then my dog died, and my mother, who was manic-depressive, was admitted to mental hospital for periods of up to six months at a time. A caring aunt, who had just lost her husband, came from New Zealand to look after me for a year. When she returned to New Zealand, I was very sad for a long time. But I had already learned to mourn alone and it may have strengthened my ability to be independent and extend my horizons. Be open to new worlds.

As a fourteen-year-old, I spent part of April with two friends in an isolated cottage in Glen Prosen, an Angus glen in the southern Grampians, with no through road. It was like a first long journey fired by an immense flush of freedom.

Iain was also fourteen and David a year younger. We fished for food and fended for ourselves. Craigiemeg Cottage sat in isolation on the mountain Ben Bouie, high above Prosen Water. The little house looked like it had been carved into the hillside. Built of stone with a slate roof, it was flanked by one rowan tree.

To get there, we had spent the best part of the day cycling from Dundee over the Sidlaw Hills, across Strathmore Valley, through Glamis and Kirriemuir, towards the Angus glens. On the last stretch up to the cottage in Glen Prosen we had to push our bikes up rabbit runs in knee-high heather, laden with basic provisions like oatcakes, cheese and honey.

The cottage had not been occupied for some time. The floors and chairs were peppered with mouse droppings. Light came from oil lamps and, once in a while, all three of us were required to carry a gas tank up the hill in a barrow to power the stove. Water was cranked up using a hand pump and the toilet was outside. We called it 'the ig-loo'. Firewood we gathered from a forest about a mile away.

There was a kitchen and living room with stone floors downstairs and a tiny bedroom off the attic upstairs, consisting only of a straw mattress which we had to share. In the living room, there was a table with an old wind-up gramophone and one 78 rpm covered in mouse droppings. The scratched record featured Spike Jones and His Wacky Wakakians playing the Hawaiian War Chant. At night, in the dim light, Iain, David and I huddled around the log fire, the wind roaring down the chimney.

Every morning we took it in turns to get our milk-can filled at the Macintosh farm across the glen. This was an expedition. To decide who would be the milk boy on the first morning, we lined up three kitchen chairs in a row and invented a masturbating competition. We were all fourteen and had just learned about this new bodily function from an older boy at school. Until then, we had never really put it to use. Never yet had the chance to kiss a girl. The boy whose sperm went furthest across the stone floor would be the first to fetch the milk from Geordie Macintosh's farm at daybreak.

Geordie's farm was about three miles across the glen. It was a speck on the hillside, often just visible through the mist. Hiking there meant holding the big milk-can high above the heather, clambering over dry stane dykes and rickety bridges and plodding through peat bogs peppered with hielan' coo pancakes, as cow dung was called in Prosen. Years later, in India, I was transported back to Prosen when I saw my name spelled on a train ticket from Varanasi to Darjeeling as Khan Milkie.

Across the moor, the wind carried the plaintive song of the peewit and the sad musical cry of the curlew who had begun to nest there. I never felt alone there. In fact, I had felt more isolated and confined in the city. There was a kind of solace in the moor, even with the rain streaking in my face. It was the rain after all that had washed my tears away the day my father died.

My arrival at the Macintosh farm was greeted by two barking collies chained to the barn wall. The door of the farmhouse was answered by Mrs Macintosh, a broad-shouldered country woman with flowing grey hair, blue-and-white flowered apron and cheeks like polished apples. She filled my can with milk from another can and introduced me to a ferret tied up in the farmyard, with a long string attached to his collar.

'That's Sandy, Geordie's ferret,' said Mrs Macintosh. 'Sandy keeps us well supplied with rabbits.'

On my journey back to the cottage, I had air cover from a hawk who was hovering in the sky high above me, probably hoping that I would disturb a field mouse. On the edge of the forest, I met a huge black capercaillie who stood enigmatically in the heather. When I passed him, he uttered a sound like someone belching into a didgeridoo. The Gaels called this big black grouse the *capull coille,* 'horse of the woods'. Capercaillies are rarely seen but I would see this one filling the frame of the little bedroom window most mornings. Perhaps I imagined it, but he always seemed to be edging closer to the cottage, as if curious.

Most days we ate trout which we fished from either the Crammie or the Logie, both tributaries of Prosen Water. In April, the rivers lashed down the rocks in spate. Iain, whose parents owned Craigiemeg as a retreat, taught me to lie on the river bank and dip my cupped hand in the icy torrent. In a matter of minutes, a trout would take shelter in my numb purple hand and could be gently lifted out of the water, without any need of hooks or worms. It was called guddling.

During this ritual, I watched a family of otters bringing fish back to their nest which was embedded in the river bank. Occasionally, the otters would stop and look at me. They seemed to realize that my aim was basically the same as theirs, only the methods were different.

In Glen Prosen, there were many days of wind and rain. Since childhood, the patter of rain on a window pane has reminded me of sad, but never hopeless times. The drips of water, like tears, are on a journey. Like rivers, they join to gain momentum. The three of us were often drenched and remained wet until we dried out in the wind.

Glen Prosen had also been the home of Dr Edward Wilson. It was in his cottage at nearby Dykehead that Wilson and Robert Falcon Scott planned their second, ill-fated, expedition to the South Pole in 1910. Scott's ship for his earlier 1902 expedition with Wilson to Antarctica was a converted wooden whaler built in Dundee, *The Discovery,* at anchor today in her birthplace. In Broughty Ferry Castle museum is a letter from Scott thanking my father's firm for sails that never let the expedition down.

My father had often told me about Scott of the Antarctic. It was with this man in my mind, perhaps even as a driving force, that I suggested we go on an expedition to climb the highest mountain in the region. There was a spirit of adventure in the Prosen air.

Around the fire at night, we talked a lot about Scott's expedition to the South Pole and, early next morning, we packed our rucksacks for an early start. Our attempted ascent of the mountain Driesh, commanding the glen to the west, did not adhere to any of the rules that should be followed in expeditions by mountaineers. We wore gym shoes and had no map, no compass, no supplies beyond oatcakes, cheese and three Mars bars. When thirsty, we drank from a burn. Of course, we should have known better. But we were fourteen and it was a sunny day. Driesh, at 3107 feet, is the highest mountain in the region. It seemed to beckon us from the head of the glen.

The winding road that follows Prosen Water expires at Runtaleave, two-thirds of the way up the glen, leaving the upper section secluded. We hiked over the hills to Runtaleave and waded through bogs and bracken to reach the lower slopes of Driesh. We were charged with energy, fired by the sun and unthreatening cotton-wool clouds whisking across the clear blue sky and dappling the mountains with light.

We carved a route through the ferns somewhere between Hunt Hill and Cairn Baddoch. Above us, we saw the broad blunt wings of a buzzard swoop on what looked like a young rabbit and carry it off. We reached the top of one ridge after the other but the higher we climbed, the less sense of the summit we had. Driesh has a short southern ridge and a long eastern saddle connecting it, via a narrow col, with the neighbouring mountain Mahar. We were losing whatever bearings we had. The sun had gone and we were now being drenched by rain and sleet. I regretted not adhering to my father's advice when I was a child: 'There's not such a thing as bad weather, Kenneth. Only the wrong clothes.'

Then, as often happens in the mountains of Scotland, a blanket of mist cloaked the mountain top and began to fold down the slopes. We had the feeling that we had been climbing but not getting any higher and were uncertain if we were going in the right direction. Hours seemed to pass. We met several herds of deer who, unlike us, seemed to know exactly where they were.

We stopped. Enveloped in cold damp mist, we waited, but were unwilling to go back down. After about an hour, the mist lifted and Iain and I decided to press on. David refused, saying we were fools. He decided to stay where he was and read John Buchan's *The Thirty-Nine Steps* which he had brought with him. Iain and I carried on up, promising to return to collect David. We decided to keep in touch as much as possible by whistling. (I had also brought along a penny whistle in my little canvas rucksack which, of course, should have contained more practical things but that whistle has a way of travelling with me.)

Up we went. It got steeper and steeper as we plodded over ridge after ridge. Then, the mist came down again as the ground began to level off. Any orientation we had, was gone. Suddenly we reached a plateau which seemed to be the highest one could go on the mountain. This was the top. But it dropped off dramatically on one side into the steep Winter Corrie ravine overlooking Glen Doll. A deep croak came from a solitary raven gliding over the ridge. When a bank of mist engulfed us again, we very nearly toppled over the edge on to scree.

I have to admit, I was enjoying every moment of this, irresponsible as that may seem. I was in my element. The passion to press on outpaced any blisters on my feet or aches in the legs. Indeed, I have always found it hard to know when to stop.

Our poor route-finding on Driesh may have set a course for me – the drive to explore became more important than reaching the peak. And that thrill of being on the edge of the unknown became addictive. The emotional gap in my life at that point in Prosen, as in my childhood, had been filled with a wild and boundless spirit of curiosity and adventure that has never dampened.

I have wallowed in difficult situations and pushed myself to the limit again and again in my travelling life. Roads reveal more when they lead through unexpected places. The destination itself is never the goal. Years later, cycling one summer with a tent along by-roads from Brittany to the Riviera, I ended up on the top of Mont Ventoux, because I had misread the Michelin map. But it led to a delirious detour.

Whether in the mountains or in the desert I am overwhelmed by an extreme feeling of freedom – a state of mind that seems to kick in on a journey like a dormant pill implanted in my past. As if a pilot light somewhere inside me ignites into energy as soon as I'm on the road.

When travelling, one's support systems fail as they did for me after my father's death. The certainties of daily existence and protection of familiarity no longer apply. But you gain momentum from the reality around you. You never feel alone. In many ways, you become a child again. You view the world with fresh eyes.

In Glen Prosen, there was something about the dominance and permanence of the surrounding mountains that commanded respect and offered a kind of security during that trip. It felt like an adventure then, but in a way it gave me strength. This was a welcome feeling. My pillars of support in life had totally fallen away. But I found refuge in Prosen with my friends. We were both challenged and united by the nature around us which we were dependent on and were a part of. But we also became more aware of ourselves in dealing with it.

While I revelled in being lost on the edge of Winter Corrie, Iain was much more sensible, tracking back and looking for a burn or a fence that would guide us down the mountain. Ultimately we found the foundations of a dry stane dyke and a burn trickling downwards. It was getting dark but the mist was lifting again.

I played my penny whistle as loud as I could but there was no response from David down the mountain, at least that we could hear. Instead, there was a rumble of cloven hooves as a flock of black-faced sheep shuffled up to me through the heather while I was playing, somewhat over-optimistically, an Irish tune *Where the grasses grow and the breezes blow in a free and easy way…* The sheep were attracted to the music and just stood there in vacant appreciation.

We kept our promise and fortunately found David. He had long completed his *Thirty-Nine Steps*. 'You stupid idiots!' he yelled. 'It's been hours. No one knew we were here. We could have all perished.' David was right of course. Understandably, he had been anxious and was angry. He had countered his fear by being rational. Iain and I didn't like giving up.

It was nightfall but fortunately the moon outlined the contours of the landscape for us. We focused on a distant yellow light twinkling from a farmhouse in the glen below. A few hours later, as dawn broke, we collapsed into the straw mattress at Craigiemeg.

Unlike Scott's last expedition, planned in this glen, our juvenile drama on Driesh had ended without fatalities. And, for me, the seeds of journeys ahead had begun to grow.

Walking the Edges

Margaret Elphinstone

I walked the map of Scotland into my memory. I've gained a different perspective from remote places that are difficult to get to – a joining of the dots. I've seen how glens connect to one another, and how the routes of the modern roads are singular and arbitrary, compared with the infinite network of possibilities open to the traveller on foot. I've learned lateral thinking on the ground.

When I read what I've written in my hill diaries over the years, I see that there are recurring themes. The search for language is one – finding a way of putting experience into words. Wilderness came long before words. Wilder creatures than me, who have no language, know the hills as I never can. The very fact I've wanted to climb these hills, and needed to write about them, is a measure of my separation from them. Maybe that's all my accounts do – express the depth of my separation. There should be sorrow in that, but the project has nearly always been one of great joy – a sense of getting back to a place that had been forgotten.

It isn't possible to go very far into wilderness in Scotland, and of course it's not an untouched wilderness. The hand of history has written over it everywhere. And yet there's a sense of proportion in the hills – a different perspective that brings its own comfort. I find myself saying 'It's so satisfying to look down where I have so often looked up.'

Time and space take on new meanings in the hills. The past sometimes moves in very close. I sit on a rock, and I think, how many people have sat just here, looking at just this, since human beings first came to Scotland? Time collapses, and those past people, although I can never know them, seem to be very near.

Many of those people knew the land far better than I ever will. They had names for things which I don't even see.

There's a sense up there of being on the edge in so many different ways: on the edge of what I can do, on the edge of what I know, on the edge of things I can't understand and have no language for. I've been delighted, thrilled, frightened, awed, amazed by weather. The mountains have let me into their world, and I'm lucky, but the time I spend up there is always borrowed. I can't live up there. We go to the hills on their sufferance, and sometimes the face they show to us is kind.

None of this would have happened if my father hadn't taught me to go to the hills in the first place. The first walk he took me – up Langstrath, over High Raise, on to Pike o' Stickle and Harrison Stickle, and down into Dungeon Ghyll – was the beginning of a lifelong journey. He showed me the way. I see him in my mind's eye: it's a fine day, he's leaning back on one elbow, the summit cairn behind him, smoking his cigarette and gazing into the blue distance, across ridge upon ridge of Lakeland hills. With his map and his Wainwright he'll work out which is which, and name every single one before we move on. He taught me to use a map and compass, and he taught me that there was something vital hidden in the names of the hills – it was somehow part of knowing them to be able to name them.

It was important for me to do this on my own. Sometimes I've had company. No one could wish for better company on the hill than I've had over the years. It was better still to be alone. Scary sometimes, but I had the satisfaction of knowing that I'd done everything – the navigation, the scrambling, the decisions, the observations, the route ... all on my own. I've written somewhere in my diaries 'Followers don't really learn much'. I know that I can manage alone on the hill. I also know what I can't do.

Whatever happens, for the rest of my life I can look up at the high places, and I'll know what it's like up there. To the end of my life I'll be able to remember when I wasn't looking up at the hills, but looking down from them. I'm as grateful as I can be that I had the chance to do this, and that I took it when I could.

The excerpts that follow are arranged by dates through the seasons; many years' walking have been collapsed into one stroll through the seasons. This telescoping of time accounts for any geographical and conceptual leaps. I want to show how, when I look back now, the years signify less and less, and the seasons matter more and more.

BEINN MHANACH: March 29th

... It's good to be travelling down an ancient road, and thinking of who must have walked down here in all the centuries before. There was no one on the road today but a fine herd of Highland cattle. I passed Duncan Ban MacIntyre's cottage at Ars an t-sSdhean. It's easy to see why Duncan wrote so much about Beinn Dorain; he really did live 'underneath the mountain'. It was interesting looking down into Glen Lyon from the col. I wonder where the monastery was that gave Beinn Mhanach its name? Under the water maybe. From the col it was a hard soggy pull north over moss and grass to the ridge, pretty steep. There was some snow lying in patches above 850 metres or so. There'd been wisps of cloud over Creag Mhor earlier, but now I could see Ben Challum, Creag Mhor, and of course a fine view of Dorain, Dothaidh, Achallader and Beinn a Creachan from the east. Not all mountains are as dramatic from every vantage point. There was cloud over Beinn Lui to the west. I walked the ridge to Beinn a Chuirn, then traversed back to the watershed, and took the long road back though a lovely afternoon. You can tell it's springtime; you can hear the birds again. Some RAF planes came over just as I reached the viaduct – a Nimrod flying very low – which was a bit of a shock.

BEN HOPE: April 14th

Storer describes the Road of Desolation in the context of the terrible history of the Sutherland clearances. Is it that we know the history, or is this landscape truly haunted? Strath More is a lovely glen, almost empty now of people, but they have left their traces very strongly. As you enter the glen you can see very clearly where the Vikings must have tracked their ships up the river into the safe Hop. Then, going further back, we went to the broch at Dun Dornaigil which guards the narrows south of the loch, where the Creags block the glen to the west. Showers blew over us, and between each one a bright window lit up the whole wilderness of Sutherland with sudden light.

SGURR ALASDAIR: April 15th

... a beautiful Alpine day, clearing to blue skies and the best long range visibility ... The Great Stone Chute was made much easier by the layer of sticky snow. The chute narrows, and suddenly we were on the ridge, just below the summit. We found three rucksacks in a hollow ... the guys ahead of us had ropes and crampons, but as Ian said, the crampons would have made the scrambling much harder. He also said, as I crawled almost on my belly over a rock: 'You know, you're *good* at this.' This makes me very happy. I know I'd have been very good in the past. All my early tree-climbing experience is very useful in the Cuillin, because ever since I was four years old I have enjoyed the sensation of air under my heels ...

The summit is tiny; just room for us. And the view was incredible, higher than all the world, perched in a place as airy as the top of a tree. We could see the Outer Isles from Barra to Ben More on North Uist, and all the islands down to Ben More on Mull in a lovely translucent light. To the east Knoydart was white with snow, and the Cuillin around us – and a good deal lower – were like etchings in black and white.

It was one of those moments when the sheer delight and exhilaration are tinted with a little fear. I'm reminded of what Alex Maddrell[1] said to me about the sea – even on the best of days there are certain places where you have to be aware of the power that could so easily turn and destroy you. You're on borrowed time in such places, that were never meant for human beings. I'm intrigued by the *newness* of the names of the Cuillin, except for what you see from below, or at sea. Why would anyone choose to go up here, before our extraordinary post-romantic urges? The Cuillin is so wild and stony, and in every way unforgiving. There's nothing comforting about it. I'm aware all the time of being on the edge – on the edge of what I can do, and on the edge of the changeable moods of the mountains. Up there on the high point of Sgurr Alasdair, it was like usurping the place of the gods, and a small part of me is scared I might get punished.

SEANA BHRAIGH: April 17th

... At 11.07 a front, which had been lowering from the south, came in, and within minutes our clear, beautiful day had vanished before the driving wind and rain. We went into the corrie, and found wild winds gusting round it. We took a bearing west on to the ridge, where the driving rain became sleet. Visibility was still surprisingly good. We reached a height at 760, and a small tarn beyond it, from which we could see it snowing over the summit. We thought carefully about going on, and reckoned that the visibility was good, and that there was a clear escape route NE off the mountain, and out of the driving SW wind. We decided it was not stupid to go on.

Just before the top we were into cloud, and overshot our cairn by about twenty feet, as we were keeping well away from the edge of the corrie, then suddenly I looked round and saw a

---

[1] Coxswain of Port St Mary lifeboat, Isle of Man.

circular walled cairn behind us. It was 2.15 p.m. We sat down in it for a couple of minutes, and shook hands: an epic!

And here I made my big mistake. I checked the bearing too hurriedly and we set off N. Suddenly we were in terrific winds and blizzard. We staggered down as much as we could, getting knocked right over all the time. Conditions were suddenly serious, and when I checked my bearing again we were heading *west* not east. I was anxious, because the weather was awful. I got us back on to the summit. We set off again, twenty paces from the edge of the corrie, then north, then east. So I thought. But we kept getting knocked over, and it was impossible to check the map. Then we found ourselves looking into an unfamiliar corrie. When I worked it out later I realised we were heading west again towards Creag Dhubh. I could see the bealach between Creag Dhubh and Seana Bhraigh to the *right*. But at the time I wasn't sure where it was. This time I was really scared. I navigated us back to the summit. I was beginning not to trust the compass – both compasses – wondered if there were mineral deposits. In retrospect, writing in the comfort and safety of the Ceilidh Place in Ullapool, I realise I was not thinking clearly enough. Remember it was impossible even to look at the map. On our second trip back to the summit the wind hurled me off my feet. I thought my hat had gone (found it in my hood later) and banged my head on a rock. I realised this was *serious*. Not in terms of survival because I knew we could get down low enough to bivouac and we were well equipped with loads of food, but serious because of extreme conditions on top making navigation very difficult, and for a while we were lost. (I remember being terribly embarrassed at the thought of mountain rescue). But I got us back to that bloody summit, as near as we could without being blown off it. We kept being blown over on sharp rocks, which was frightening. This time I made damn sure to keep close enough to the edge of the corrie to know where it was (though being very careful because of the gusts of wind). We almost crawled down – and then I saw the tarn. I've never been so pleased to see a tarn in my whole life...

MEALL NAN EUN: April 29th

I started from Coiletur, leaving the path just before Allt Caitlin and heading Southeast up the shoulder on to Beinn Chaorach. I was very tired, and thinking too much about things I'd left behind, but when I got on to the ridge, I thought of where Christian reaches the top of the hill Difficulty and his burden rolls off his back. I wasn't thinking of sin – don't believe in any of that – so much as responsibility and pressure to be indoors and do too much. Anyway, it rolled off and bounced down the hill, and I had a good easy walk up to the summit. Having got myself in mind of *The Pilgrim's Progress* I found myself thinking about pilgrimage, and reciting Raleigh's 'Give me my scallop shell of quiet...' to myself, and then bits of *The Canterbury Tales* '... then longen folke to go on pilgrimage'. This walking is my kind of pilgrimage.

DEVIL'S POINT: May 13th

...All day long the clouds were shifting and changing. We watched lots of snow showers passing over the central Cairngorms, and sometimes to west and south of us as well, but we walked through the middle and never caught a drop of anything. But now an icy north wind came over the lip of Coire Uaine, and when we looked down Lochan Uaine was frozen solid, with amazing patterns inside the ice as one looked right into its depths from above. We walked beside a fine unbroken cornice to the summit (3 p.m.), where we found no angels, but no wind either, so we stopped for an extra coffee so we could go on admiring the astonishing corries of Braeriach. Then we traversed the SW slopes of Cairn Toul, and stopped for a while above the col to sit and take in the wild view to the south. Mike found a brave solitary violet at his feet.

While we'd been sitting all the other walkers had left the hill and there was an empty, evening feel – wild and quiet – a privilege for us to be there. It was a very easy walk up to Devil's Point. It had looked so small from the great summits, but my God it's spectacular, with its sheer drops into the Lairig and Geusachan – a very potent Devil after all! We hung about, looking east, and when we stood up, (around 5 p.m.) we noticed great grey clouds rolling in from the SW. We got off the ridge just as hailstones began to fall, and went down fast while the hailstones thickened and turned into uncompromising rain.

AN GEARANACH, STOB COIRE A'CHAIRN, AM BODACH, SGURR A' MHAIM: May 15th

...we came in by the Water of Nevis gorge, and across a little hidden meadow, and over the wire bridge to the foot of the Steall waterfall. It was ideal walking weather – not the oppressive heat of the last couple of days, but fresh and a hint of change in the air, but excellent visibility and dry. I'd woken at 5.30 to the sound of rain, and even though we were going out I could feel the relief in the air, and in my body, that the weather change had come. It was a fairly steep pull up on to An Gearanach. As we came over the shoulder just below the summit we could see the whole of the Ring of Steall, looking quite out of this world – more Icelandic than Scottish in some ways. It gave one a real sense of that other country, the landscape one always hopes to step into, and sometimes, on rarer days, one does...

CARN AN FHIDHLEIR, AN SGARSOCH: May 22nd

...I was very aware, this weekend, of how the modern roads have shaped our view of the hills. 'Remote' and 'neighbouring' take on quite different shades of meaning when one imagines the hills without the roads. Just as the Angus glens were all throughways, with nothing special to raiders or drovers about Glen Shee in particular, so too the walk from Glen Tilt, via White Bridge to Linn of Dee, is just as good a highway as the route of the A9. And Beinn Dearg and Carn a Chlamain are not on the edge of things, they are part of an open, rolling, generously scaled landscape of wide hills and big skies. Everything begins to fit together, and the human world – a glimpse of a green glen, a solitary ruin, a single tent – shrinks to its just proportions. These hills have more wildlife too, than some: too many deer, but also: frogs, lizards, even a slowworm, snipe, wheatear, lots of parti-coloured ptarmigan. The hares are all brown now except their tails and hind feet – transformation must start at the front. The flowers are just coming out – lots of violets, daisies, dandelions in the glens, and violets and wood anemones quite high up. The butterworts are almost out, and the high tops are bright with moss campion just unfurling. In spite of the snow on the Cairngorms, and a sharp NW wind blowing, this is springtime. The glens are lush, and the hills open and friendly – for the moment.

CARN BHAC, BEINN IUTHARN MHOR, AN SOCACH: May 23rd

... Glen Ey is a perfect U-shaped valley with a flat flood plain at the bottom, very green. The upper reaches were full of red deer at their early grazing, but they lolloped off in droves as we came in – same thing again in the evening when we disturbed them at their late supper. This kind of landscape, with the deer grazing, always seems to me to be primeval. Such a short time ago (7000 years just here, maybe?) there were no humans here, and in a far shorter time, I imagine, they'll all have gone. In the eighteenth century this glen was probably as full as it could hold. The green places will be far better for our absence, except who will be there to look and find them beautiful?

MULLACH NA DHEIRAGAIN: June 6th

...These mountains feel like true wilderness, and yet, in the glens, one is constantly aware of the people who are no longer there, who've left ruins and the lines of field systems, and maybe something else, a sense of habitation. You can see it in the lush grass and nettles and buttercups around the old houses. Later I looked at the Chisholm monument at the entrance to Loch Mullardoch, made up of stones from all the places – Australia, Canada etc – where Chisholms have gone, and a word about the Chisholm Trail. Their absence has left a wilderness, and people like me, who do not belong to these glens, enjoy it as if it were primeval territory. But it is not...

MEALL NAN CEAPRAICHEAN, BEINN DEARG, CONA MHEALL: June 17th

...The Web of White Stones is a wonderful name for a hill, and Eididh nan Clach Geala lives up to it. All day long on the Deargs we were struck by the bands of white quartzite, often in broad stripes across the hills like landing signals for Martians. The walk on to Meall nan Ceapraichean was an interesting descent down shattered, twisty rock formations to the lochans and up again. A few drops of rain fell as we crossed the summit ridge between the Top and Ceapraichean itself. These are very distinctive loaf-shaped hills, with fascinating rock formations and cliffs on their steep sides, and impressive views of each from all the others. There's a lot of water about in interesting little lochans, owing to the broken nature of the ground, with outcrops and hollows. Beinn Dearg is of course the king of them all, and the view from every side is deeply impressive. It's a pleasant climb up by a massive wall; one wonders if one can see it from outer space like the other Great Wall; it's certainly pretty intrusive from all other angles. Most walls blend in to their landscape. This one is a great horizontal slash across the upper reaches of the hill. Anyway, it's a pleasant walk, again over rounded boulders (a lot of that today) which are easy to negotiate, on to a glorious summit. We could see every detail of the Fannichs – many fine memories there – and spent quite a while working out the ranges further south. We could see everything – An Teallach, of course, Fisherfield, Torridon, right down to Luinnhe Beinn in the far distance.

In these conditions everything looks (and is) very accessible, and it would have been a crime not to have included Cona Mheall ... a rewarding summit, as suddenly the mountain falls away in a tremendous drop to Allt a Chrom Uilt. We could see well into mamba[2] country, up Gleann Beg and Gleann Mor (exciting names they have round here). There is nothing human until one reaches Strathcarron, whose upper reaches were visible in the distance. One wonders who once lived in these glens, knew far more names than still exist on the OS maps, and who called these wild places home.

MAM SODHAIL, CARN EIGHE, BEINN FHIONNLAIDH: June 20th

... we came to the old Ordnance Survey shelter, complete with remains of a potbellied cast-iron stove and an ancient frying pan. Who carried that lot up here? I guess they may have used ponies. We reached the amazing summit cairn in thick mist, and I climbed up and had a look inside. It looks like a Neolithic burial cairn that got misplaced. The early days of the Ordnance Survey must have been much more adventurous than photogrammetry.

... the cloud suddenly lifted and we had a stunning view of the traverse across to Carn Eighe, and Carn Eighe itself looking hugely formidable in wreathing cloud. I was suddenly aware of our temerity. Who do we think we are, trudging up to all

---

[2] Mamba = miles and miles of bugger all.

these summits? Mountains are unconquerable, and when people thought the gods lived up there, in a curious way they were not entirely wrong. Ironic that from this bastion of mapmaking I should so clearly have it borne in upon me that the high hills are immeasurable, not in metres but in mood.

When we first got to the top I hurried to a small outcrop to the NW to get a sighting of Beinn Fhionnlaidh, in case it disappeared by the time we left. There it was, almost lost in veils of mist below us. ... It may look small from the giant to its south, but deceives with many false summits, before one reaches the cairn. The oddest sight, in all those miles and miles of wilderness, is a neatly framed view of the Skye Bridge. It made me think – there seemed such a lot to think of, all day – about the way we do things now, and the way these glens were when they weren't wilderness at all. All the time I've been in Glen Affric I've been thinking of 8000 years of human history, and the marks of the ice, which only left a little time before that, and before that... These mountains were all made when two great plates of land collided. Sometimes I sit on a summit, and I wonder who, if anyone, in the last eight thousand years, has sat in that exact same place on that rock. Those people of the past feel closer in high places, because although human history has changed, and changed the land, it has not changed the shapes of hills or sea.

BEN AVON: LEABAIDH AN DAIMH BHUIDHE, BEINN A'BHUIRD: June 21st

... This is an extraordinary plateau, quite unlike anywhere else I've been in Scotland. The rock formations are like Monument Valley in the Arizona desert, but the hills are green and blue, not red. Ben Avon is a remote, primeval place. It wouldn't be surprising to meet a dinosaur – at least, I would be surprised, but it would seem less inappropriate than a saurian monster at, say, Ballater station. The rock formations are like monster's droppings, anyway. One sees these strange pimples from far away – on Bynack Mhor, on Beinn Mheadhoin too – they seem to have landed where they are by chance ... I managed to climb the rock to the real summit (about six inches higher than the easy scramble).

We set off west across the Sneck and up on to Beinn A' Bhuird. We reached another outcrop just north of Cnap a' Chleirich, and there the mist began to close in. We took a bearing and reached North Top, but there was nothing on the ground but a sad cairn, and no visibility, so we didn't hang about. We took a (slightly disputed) bearing back to the edge of Garbh Choire, and the mist cleared at about 1000 metres. This was incentive enough to send me back up on to Stob an t-Sluichd, a most attractive top with a scaly back like a brontosaurus. We came down pretty much due north in to Glen Avon, then back to the bikes. It was a golden evening, and being midsummer's night we felt no anxiety about time: a great freedom. Once we were on the downhill stretch to Delnadamph, and then on the tarmac road to Corgarff, we fairly whizzed along – a wild night ride it was. We reached Jenny's Bothy just after 10 p.m. Ben Avon is the nearest you can get on Earth to leaving the planet, I reckon, a very suitable enterprise for midsummer's night.

SLIOCH June 23rd

... it's cathedral in scale – much larger than any man-made thing, in fact, but the sense of scale and the acoustics are like a cathedral. Slioch is a three-tiered mountain, and each layer is different. The lower slopes above the burn are open, then the corrie and the ridge surrounding it is like being inside a volcano crater (I know it isn't one, but it reminds me of the great craters in the Azores). Then the highest layer is like the Sheep Craig on Fair Isle – the same horseshoe-shaped slab of rock with precipices all round, except for the steep slope we came up by. It was a stiff pull out of the corrie – very hot – with a welcome breeze on the ridge, and all the views of Beinn Eighe and Liathach to the south opening out across Loch Maree in front of us. Then up to the main plateau of Slioch, scrambly at first then slog over grass. Slioch has a false summit, with a trig point on it – imagine thinking in mist that you'd made the top, and realising after you got down that it hadn't been the top at all ... The real summit is a little further west, and the ridge is very like a Shetland cliff walk, with the drop to the left of you. We spent quite a bit of time on the summit, looking all around us, then took the super ridge walk – one of the very best – round the corrie to Sgurr an Tuill Bhain. We took it slowly as there is so much to look at. Once again we were able to retrace every step of our long walk into Fisherfield two days ago, and it was good to see A'Mhaighdean and Ruadh Stac Mor, as we hadn't been able to see much when we were on them. An Teallach dominates everything to the north. It's the last bastion of these wonderful mountains, and it's a stunner.

BEN MACDUI, CARN A'MHAIM, DERRY CAIRNGORM: June 24th

In the high Cairngorms, perhaps even more than in the other mountains of Scotland, one is aware one is here on sufferance. Today was a bright midsummer's day; the signs are still everywhere that this is essentially an un-human place. You can see the bare stretches and darkened grass where the snow has lain until late. There is still snow in the high corries. The precipices across the Lairig Ghru are fearsome; the distances are long.

We cycled to Derry Lodge from Linn of Dee, and left the bikes by the bridge. Then we walked up Glen Luibig as far as the shoulder of Carn a'Mhaim, and started climbing north. From the summit we looked into the Lairig Ghru. And ghru it is, even on a fine summer's day. We saw snow buntings which were to become a regular sight over the next few days. They reminded me of staying at the Strutslaug hut above Myrdalsjokull in Iceland. The flowers were similar to Iceland too – lots of moss campion even in the most barren places, just like Maellifellsandur. A fine ridge walk, with stunning views of the Lairig Ghru, took us off Carn a'Mhaim, down quite a drop, and then we started the long haul up Ben McDui, over boulders that seemed as if they'd only tumbled down last week. It's a landscape that makes one feel very small – a mouse running across the floor of the giant's kitchen.

We were standing on the roof of Scotland, and on such a day that we could see it all. I won't list it. It's all there on the monument at the top, and if anyone needs to know what you can see from the summit of Ben Macdui you can go up there and read it. But that day we *could* see everything it mentioned, from the Pentlands to Ben Hope. You stand there, and the whole country is spread out round you. It's the map come alive, which shows that in my experience the text has often come before the place. True of Ben Macdui anyway; I read it long before I saw it or stood on it. Some of what I have read did not seem to be here. Mike reckons the Grey Man is just the brokenspectre, which I've seen already, on Cruachan and on Ben Lawers, and it wasn't in the least frightening. Adam Watson is more respectful – or gullible? At midsummer, in perfect weather, the mountain was a giant asleep. I felt like Jack come up the beanstalk. I didn't want a golden harp, but I got what I did want – and I didn't get punished for it. You can still respect what's there, even if you're one of the lucky ones.

BEINN MHEADHOIN, BEINN BHREAC, BEINN A'CHAORAINN: June 6th

...It was so hot I had thoughts of flinging myself into Loch

Etchachan, and being able to say I'd gone swimming at over 3000 feet, but I didn't quite manage it. I waded in deep which was refreshing, but chill. From the loch it's an easy route on to Beinn Mheadhoin, another eerie primeval landscape. We went to both tops, and wandered like Lilliputians among the weird rock formations. The views down into Loch Avon were very wild, and redolent of rock climbing history – looking at the Shelter Stone – but also of aeons of time before that. Not a place where much changes, except rockfalls and avalanches. Plenty of snow buntings again; they begin to seem very familiar.

...These mountains are bigger than Ben Lui, but quite dwarfed when you look down on them from Ben Macdui. It's a huge sweep of landscape, and distances are very deceptive, even with a map telling you the truth. I like it; all so bare and open...

BEINN BHEOIL: July 8th

Cloud low and solid, but fine underneath it, so planned a low level walk to Loch Ericht to find Cluny Macpherson's cave by Benalder Lodge. A walk full of life – must have seen, during the day, upwards of two hundred deer, almost as ubiquitous as the frogs. A dipper on the burn. A slowworm by the path. Rampant flowers – marsh orchids, tormentil, lousewort, milkwort, orchids, alpine lady's mantle, moss campion, slender Saint John's wort, bedstraw, the first bell heather, a thing with delicate yellow trumpets (this is not according to habitat but random memory). Was pottering about with no success – dammit, if David Balfour could find the bloody cave, so should I be able to – along the loch shore, searching the crags. (It says in *Kidnapped* that it's above a steep wood under a crag – not a vestige of a wood in sight, *plus ca change* I suppose) when the mist lifted like a miracle, so I headed for up. View from Sron na Iolaire amazing, from Beinn Bheoil outstanding – everything from Dalwhinnie to Ben Nevis, the Great Wall of Rannoch, Schiehallion, Loch Ericht navy blue and mysterious down below.

SGURR MHIC CHOINNICH: July 12th

It wasn't actually raining as Iain and I tramped up to Coire Lagan in nil visibility, but as we started climbing up the unremitting scree it soon made up for that. There was one magic moment as we passed the lochan, which truly looked as if it might reveal a hand clothed in white samite, mystic, wonderful – it was an Excalibur sort of day. But that was about it. We reached the six foot wide ridge, and saw nothing, but felt a mighty rushing wind. Actually it was never really cold; the heatwave temperatures must have been just above the clouds. I was soaked to the skin, but there was little wind and I wasn't in the least chilled. At least I'd seen the ridge in all its glory from Sgurr Alasdair – I knew what kind of place I was in, but the cloud was so close there wasn't even an impression of the huge drop on both sides. There were some difficult steps along the ridge, made a lot worse by being wet. The gabbro is great but the basalt is as sliddery as ice in places. I got the usual crop of Cuillin bruises on my knees; I don't think my technique can be that great.

As I've found before in the Cuillin, I was still expecting more challenges when suddenly the summit was there. It's very small and mostly taken up by a cairn with a 1950s memorial slab in it. I don't want a memorial stone on a mountain, please. They're both intrusive and dispiriting, and I doubt if the people commemorated were either of those things. There were signs of life on the summit too. A starry saxifrage had seeded itself right by the cairn. There were alpine ladies' mantle and grass, and, surprisingly, a healthy bramble shoot. A bird must have shat a blackberry pip...

CISTE DHUBH: July 25th

... It took an hour to get to the bealach, which is a curious kind of ante-room between the hills, and then it was a lovely open ridge walk to the top, with imposing bastions of rock to the east. Quite a few deer. Wonderful view into Glen Affric, and I was able to identify all the Affric and Kintail Munros, right up into the Mullardoch wilderness. It draws me in, that place, but there's no time this year, as the stalking season begins next week. I stayed a while on the top and watched the evening shadows and the gold light on the hills. Walked back over Am Bathach. Strange experience going up; a kind of vision, a sort of prefiguring of death as something joyful. It's the old *déjà vu* of the ridge and the blue sky, an open space ahead, a sort of exultation and a freedom. Never tried to write this down before. But it was there, a kind of heaven in Kintail. The ridge was bigger than it looked, and the evening growing late, all the valleys in shadow down below, but up there the sun not yet set. It was sad to come down, back to the valley things.

SGURR CHOINNICH, SGURR A'CHAORACHAIN: August 1st

The views all day were wonderful, and I had a sense of being right in the middle of the highland hills – an epicentre, not a remote outpost. More and more I realise how the Wade road system, and the effect of our modern communications network, has distorted our view of the Highland glens, and the multifarious ways through, where once there were thriving communities and all sorts of communication between them. But to get up high in glorious weather, and see everything from An Teallach to Sgritheall, from the Cuillin (though they disappeared later as the haze grew) to Ben Wyvis, is an amazing expansion of perspectives.

I have now looked at the Mullardoch hills from every angle, and seen far more of them than I ever did when I was on them.

For that reason I'm keen to go back. But the lifting of the cloud is symbolic as well as literal. I have spent hours learning how all these hills join up, and getting a sense of the whole lie of the land. Whereas when I went to Mullardoch five years ago I had no notion of all the hills round me, now I can stand on a summit and name everything, and after I've taken one or two bearings all the new angles fall into place, and I can see how all the ranges fit together. Why does this fascinate me so? I don't just do it in the hills. I'm the same with the islands: I was doing exactly the same on *Halton*[3] two weeks ago. I know little geology, geomorphology, zoology, botany etc, and only a modicum of history. But the simple act of being able to picture the land correctly gives me intense pleasure, and I learn scraps of geography, in all its aspects, as this helps me elucidate the land I'm interested in. I suppose it comes out in the novels too. It must all be about *something*. I've spent so long creating this image of the land in my head, and yet it will die with me. I suppose the point is that it makes me happy.

The ranges upon ranges of hills, basking in the primeval sun, were almost overwhelming, as if I had stepped right out of human time, and could see how the glaciers had so recently melted away, and now things were changing again. Sunshine in late summer seems so old, not like the young sun in spring; it seems to bear all its millions of years and make one's own memories both small and very vivid at the same time.

BRAERIACH August 28th

...we skirted Coire Bhrochan up to the summit. The views were full of memories for Mike, as he'd camped in An Garbh Choire in 1965 when he was working on a snow-monitoring project. Now there is no snow to be seen; the last permanent

---

[3] MV Halton, Stromness.

snows of Scotland were in the Braeriach corries. This summer would have finished them off if any were left at all. I have been quite melancholy this summer, deep down, about the state of this poor sad planet, and what we have done. It has been so all my life, but too much is coming true. John and I talked about it when we were sitting on the summit of Sgorr Nan Coireachan, and he said that beautiful though it was, we had seen almost no wildlife, no birds. There are more flowers and birds in the eastern hills than the west. I'm thinking back to last month when I was with the bird ringers on Sule Skerry and North Rona, and then back in Shetland and Fair Isle. Just seeing the seabirds in those places lifts my heart. I know they too are under threat. But in the islands – same on the Isle of May at Easter – you enter this primeval world of another form of life. It's wilderness, just as the mountains are, but inhabited by its own kind. (What is wilderness, after all? Only places where people are not.) And the habitations of the mountains seem now to be so empty. I know I haven't a good eye, and don't always see what others would see, but I recognise a lack of abundance that should not be. It isn't because it's high or marginal – after all, I have spent quite a lot of time, all told, in the Arctic tundra, and there was no sense of waste land there. (But our Lapland expedition, of course, was before Chernobyl.)

AN STUC Sept 4th

I didn't see much of the famed vegetation of Ben Lawers though the autumn colours are lovely, the hills all red and brown. I must come back in spring and find the pre-Ice-Age flowers (Ben Lawers was a nunatak). The bilberries were just in time; a hundred feet higher and I'd hit the snow line. The weather was fantastic, cold and windy, with sleet showers and scudding clouds, and wonderful windows opening up between. I don't suppose Keats had seen this, but to me it exemplifies *charm'd magic casements, opening on the foam Of perilous seas, in faery lands forlorn.* He was in Scotland, maybe he was thinking of the same thing, partly, at least. From the summit I could see scraps of Glen Lyon, little green patches far away. As I came down An Stuc reared up like a tower in front, with mist swirling over it and vanishing again.

I had my lunch on the spiky summit of An Stuc in thick mist, and while I ate my apple it cleared like a curtain going up before the play, so there was the whole toothy edge of Ben Lawers, and the east ridge going down showing my way home. Although it was snowy the path was still clear, so it was easy to go on. There were wonderful views over Glen Lyon, and back across Loch Tay, though thick black cloud was looming further north and west, and coming my way pretty fast. It hit when I was about a hundred feet below the summit, and I did the last part in blizzard. It's a nice feeling to reach a top that's familiar, and see it looking different. Last time the sheltered spaces were full of snow; this time the bones of rock were jutting through. It wasn't too cold, so I hung about while the shower passed, and was rewarded by more stunning views. And better: just as I was leaving I saw the *whole* brockenspectre. I realise now the one I saw on Cruachan was just the outer ring. That was there again: a big circle of bright white surrounding me just to the north. The sun was shining from the south; there was a big blackish blizzard cloud to my north, and there against it, inside the white halo, I could see a little circular rainbow, and myself inside it, a shadow that jumped about and waved just when I did. It left me as I started going down. I hope I find it waiting for me at 3000 feet again. It obviously prefers to be high up; I see it as the bit of me that comes alive at 3000 feet or so. Even when I don't see her, she's up there inside her rainbow, I suppose, waiting for me.

BEN VANE: Nov 11th

Ben Vane = Middle Hill, which it is. A lovely golden autumn day, part of the glorious spell we've had – a real Indian summer. As I walked along to Loch Sloy I met a man from Troon, who was doing Ben Vorlich. He'd done Ben Vane, and he told me to find God's armchair when I got to the summit – a rock formation where God could sit looking south and admire his handiwork. The information was like having a crock of gold put into my hands. Up I went, on a pleasant path that picked its way through the rocks on the eastern scarp. Behind me the view opened out across Loch Lomond, Loch Arklet, all the Rob Roy country. And when I got the summit there was all the west too – right down to Arran, Ben More on Mull, Cruachan to the north-west, the Ben Lui range, everything. I found God's armchair just a little way southwest of the summit. He had a fine day to contemplate Creation, and so did I. I went down after a leisurely lunch and a long look round; I guess he stayed.

CRUACH ARDRAIN, BEINN TULAICHEAN: Nov 19th

... Ben More and Stob Binnean were looking their snowswept best, and, just like last week, there were all the mountains round, from Ben Lawers to the east to Cruachan in the west. Also Mull and the Paps of Jura. And inimitable Ben Nevis to the north as always, with a puff of cloud over it; otherwise the day was clear as a bell. Beinn Tulaichean seemed very near indeed, and at 1.30 I reckoned I had enough daylight, so I did the ridge across in half an hour, which gave me time to enjoy the view down Glen Voil for a bit when I got there. I had to go back almost to the summit to pick up my path down. The sun was dropping fast, the evening chill coming in from the west, and the sky turning a wonderful streaky pink. I'd timed it just right, and found time to sit down for a bit. The evening was so silent. And suddenly I was surprised by one of those moments of perfect peace, a reminder and a gift. Whatever lives up here is generous as well as cold, sometimes.

BEINN A CHLEIBH: Dec 18th

... It was turning into one of those magic frosty evenings, and by the time we were back among the trees it was beginning to get dark. Tom happened to look back, and said 'Look!' There was a thin glowing line along the top of Ben Lui. We watched and it grew bigger, and then gradually a gleaming egg began to be born out of the summit of Ben Lui. It was the moon, nearly full, but it truly was egg-shaped. The birth happened quite slowly, and the egg grew and grew, then suddenly it was floating free, not an egg at all, but a nearly round fully fledged moon with an adult face. But no one can change my cosmology now I've seen it. The moon is born out of Ben Lui, and no one would ever know that who had not been standing there by Eas Damh in the right place at the right time. So I was lucky.

A Dub in Assynt

Andrew Greig

I cannot remember now where that lochan was, so small it was what my father called a *dub*. A pond, a pool, a puddle. I doubt if I could find it again. The photo shows a densely wooded slope in the background, an unidentifiable ridge rising in the distance, so it must have been fairly low down.

Possibly it is by the lovely single track road that winds and dips out of Lochinver to Clachtoll and Stoer, for there is some woodland there.

Or maybe it is somewhere near Glencanisp Lodge, off the dead-end road that turns into the track that leads below Suilven, right through to Elphin.

Or it could be found on the road which that day and on many others seemed the most beautiful – that is the simplest word, I'm afraid, for that quality that comes in through the eyes to hit where the ribs divide, making us gasp involuntarily – road in Scotland. I mean the narrow, humble, unnumbered road that unspools, elliptical and unhurried as a Sorley Maclean sentence, from Lochinver past Inverkirkaig where MacCaig spent so many summers, where AK MacLeod lived and died, then twisting, rising, falling, hiding and revealing bays, inlets, lochans, past the two houses at Rhegreanoch, on over the hill where you may crick your neck trying keep an eye on the road and look simultaneously upon Enard Bay on one side and the multi-faceted glittering sprawl of Loch Sionascaig on the other, then down to Badnagyte on the long drift to Achiltibuie and the Summer Isles.

One of the very best things about the world is that so little of it is me.

The dub I sat beside could have been in any of these places, for I passed them all that day, filling my eyes with light and water, bays and mountains, rain, rainbows and sunshine, colour from darkest slate to acidic lime green. I would not have thought there was room enough inside, for so much to come in through the eyes.

The little lochans of Assynt are sprinkled over the moor like bits of a broken windshield. Many bear water lilies; when they flower I think of miniature white lotus blooms, images of a particularly Scottish enlightenment, small, discreet, intense.

There are only so many of them you can bear to pass by. I got out of the car, that much I remember, with no purpose in mind.

I sat on a dry rock, opened my flask, peeled back a chocolate biscuit bar. Sitting out of the breeze, the sun was warm on my neck and arms, multiplied itself on the ruffled water. Pink rock orchids shook among coarse, spindly grass. A strew of small boulders, moss-blotched, scattered in the shallows. In the middle, a tiny island sprouted a single spindly rowan sapling.

It was not just the sight, but the smell. The feel. The sound.

I would say it was silent but it was not. Wind and water can never be silent. I would say – and probably did to myself, so habituated are we – that the world stopped, but it was more that, like a slow-turning roundabout in the park, I finally got on it.

For a long time, the kind that makes Time a nonsense or a friend, I sat there.

There was scalding tea, chocolate biscuit, warm arms, clouds moving in the sky and on water. There were clumps of slim reeds like green aerials. When the wind gusted, they leaned, sprung back, leaned again. They drew me into their green quivering till only the reeds and their moving remained.

(You have known that kind of looking, in childhood at least, deep in a cornfield staring at the sway, the tiny bugs close up on stalks.)

The reeds quivered and leaned, aerials responding to unseen transmissions. The air was full of transmission, in the wind itself, in radio signals, gamma rays, background radiation. In history too, coming off that low rickle of stones above the far bank. The future may have been signalling back as well, for some mind-blown cosmologists suggest Time may move in more than one direction.

The reeds bent and received them all, as I did.

And like aerials, the reeds transmitted as well as received. In their shiver and whip, they sent out energy. They took the wind and passed it on, slightly altering the world, slightly altered by it, irrevocably in it, like ourselves.

I sat there long past my tea going cold, riddled with Assynt, feeling that little dub flow into and out of me with every breath, every heartbeat and flicker of the eye; receiver and transmitter, actor and audience, for once I assented without reservation.

Today I write about it, which is not the same, and you read, which is not the same. And yet. And yet we bend in the wind, moving along the street among our fellow nodding aerials, transmitting and receiving, and in the thinking of it a lightness comes again.

Contributor Biographies

Robert MacFarlane

Robert Macfarlane's first book *Mountains of the Mind: A History of a Fascination* (Granta: 2003), won The Guardian First Book Award, The Sunday Times Young Writer of the Year Award, and a Somerset Maugham Award, and was filmed by the BBC. *Original Copy: Plagiarism and Originality in the Nineteenth Century*, a monograph study of Victorian ideas of literary property and propriety, was published by Oxford University Press in 2007. *The Wild Places* – a travelogue exploring the histories and landscapes of 'the wild' in Britain and Ireland – was published by Granta in September 2007, and won The Boardman-Tasker Prize for Mountain Literature, and the Scottish Arts Council Non-Fiction Book of the Year Award. It is presently being adapted by the BBC's Natural History unit for an hour-long film. Robert Macfarlane also writes on literature, travel, and the environment for *The Guardian* and *The Times Literary Supplement*, among other publications.

Gerry Loose

Gerry Loose is a poet. His words are as likely to be found inscribed in gardens & wild landscapes as on the page. In 2006 he was awarded a Robert Louis Stevenson Fellowship to stay in Hotel Chevillon at the edge of the Forest of Fontainebleau, and a Creative Scotland Award to live in and to study and write about the Sunart oakwoods for a year – where *Ardnamurchan Almanac* was written. He has been Poet in Residence at Glasgow's Botanic Gardens and at Jardin des Plantes, Montpellier. His publications include *the deer path to my door* (Oystercatcher Press); *that person himself* (Shearsman); *From Kyoto to Carbeth: poems & exhibition catalogue* (Collins / SPL 2008); *Ten Seasons: explorations in Botanics* (Luath / SPL) 2007; *Printed on Water: New & Selected Poems* (Shearsman Books) 2007; *Seed Catalogue* (Yorkshire Sculpture Park) 2006; *Eitgal* (Mariscat) 2001; *Tongues of Stone* (Mariscat) 1998; *a measure* (Mythic Horse) *1996* & *The Elementary Particles* (Taranis) 1993.

Neil Hegarty

Neil Hegarty was born in Derry in 1970. He is the author of *Dublin: A View from the Ground* (Piatkus, 2007); and of *The Story of Ireland*, which is forthcoming from BBC Books. His journalism has appeared in the *Irish Times* and *Daily Telegraph*, and his short fiction in the *Warwick Review* and *Stinging Fly*. His website is www.neilhegarty.com.

Marco Daane

Marco Daane is Dutch, born in 1959 and works as an editor. As a writer he specialises in literary history, nowadays mainly British. He's a member of the board of editors of the Dutch journal *De Parelduiker (The Pearl Diver)*, covering all matters of literary history. His books include *De vrijheid nog veroveren ('To conquer freedom')*, a biography of the Flemish poet Richard Minne (2001) and *Een eigen koninkrijk ('A kingdom of his own')*, a combination of travelogue, biography and history dealing with six islands and authors (2008).

Kenneth Taylor

Kenneth Taylor writes and presents nonfiction based on wildlife, science, culture and history for a variety of media. This includes magazines such as *BBC Wildlife, Country Living* and *National Geographic,* and scripts and interviews for television and radio. His seven books include *Natural Heartlands*, which was short-listed for the international BP/ Natural World prize. He has carried out research on seabirds on several islands of the St Kilda group and on other Scottish outliers. Also a photographer and musician, he lives on the Black Isle.

Michelle Cotter

Michelle Cotter is from Dublin but now lives, works and studies on the Isle of Skye. She has a PhD in anthropology, specialising in culture and the environment, and has written articles and reviews on this subject. She spends her spare time exploring the Highlands on foot or two wheels, never without a notebook! This is her first piece of non-fiction prose, revisiting some of those notebooks collected over many years – and miles – in the north-west of Ireland.

Mandy Haggith

Mandy Haggith first studied Philosophy and Mathematics and then Artificial Intelligence. A decade ago she left academia to pursue a life of writing and revolution, and has since travelled all over the world researching forests and the people dependent on them and campaigning for their protection. She has an M. Phil in Creative Writing from Glasgow University. A pamphlet of her poetry, *letting light in*, was published in 2005. Her first full collection of poetry, *Castings*, was published by Two Ravens Press in February 2007 and her first novel, *The Last Bear,* also by Two Ravens Press in March 2008. In 2008 Virgin Books published her book about the impacts of runaway paper consumption: *Paper Trails: From Trees To Trash – the true cost of paper.* Mandy lives on a woodland croft in Assynt.

Jane Alexander

Jane Alexander is a novelist and short story writer living in Edinburgh. She is a graduate of Edinburgh College of Art and the University of Glasgow M.Phil course in Creative Writing, and the recipient of a Scottish Arts Council New Writers' Bursary.

Lisa Samson

Lisa Samson's first short story was published in *Brand Literary Magazine* last year and she has recently completed her first novel. She has an MA in Creative Writing from the University of Leeds and teaches English part-time in the School of Cultural Studies at Leeds Metropolitan University. In the Autumn of 2009, she started her PhD in Creative Writing. She has had a number of short plays performed in Yorkshire theatres.

Alison Grant

Alison Grant is a freelance landscape planner who has also trained as a fine artist and undertaken creative writing courses run by the Open University. She was brought up on a farm in Angus, and has lived much of her life in rural Scotland. She has written technical publications about landscape and landscape management, but this is her first published piece of literary writing.

Raja Shehadeh

Raja Shehadeh is the author of *When the Bulbul Stopped Singing* and *Strangers in the House*. A Palestinian lawyer and writer who lives in Ramallah, he is a founder of the pioneering human rights organisation, Al-Haq, an affiliate of the International Commission of Jurists, and the author of several books about international law, human rights and the Middle East. In 2008 he was awarded the Orwell Prize for Political Writing for *Palestinian Walks*.

Judith Thurley

Judith Thurley was born and raised in County Down, on the shore of Belfast Lough. After taking a degree in languages, she trained as a nurse in the Belfast City Hospital. Her pamphlet *Listening for Hedgehogs* was published by Lapwing Press in 1995, and her work has been published in Ireland, Canada and the U.S. She is the author of 'The Enchanted Way', a chapter of *A Natural History of Ulster*, and she is currently preparing her next collection of poetry for publication.

Lesley Harrison

Lesley Harrison grew up in Angus, and after many years of wandering now lives in Orkney where she is a primary school teacher. Her poems have appeared in various magazines and anthologies. Her first pamphlet, *Sea Stories*, won a NLS Callum MacDonald award. Her second, *One Bird Flying*, based on her year in Mongolia and the journals of Marco Polo, was published in 2009 by Mariscat Press.

Sara Maitland

Sara Maitland is a novelist and short story writer. Born in 1950, she grew up in SW Scotland and studied at Oxford University. Her first novel, *Daughters of Jerusalem*, was published in 1978 and won the Somerset Maugham Award. This has been followed by several more novels and collections of short stories – most recently *Far North* and other dark tales (Maia Press 2008). She also writes non-fiction: in 2008 Granta published *A Book of Silence*. She was recently named in *The Guardian*'s list of 'the one hundred most important women public intellectuals' and lives in splendid solitude on a high moor in western Galloway.

Susan Richardson

Susan Richardson is a writer, performer and educator based in Wales. Her collection of poetry, *Creatures of the Intertidal Zone* (Cinnamon Press) was inspired by her journey through Iceland, Greenland and Newfoundland in the footsteps of an eleventh-century female Viking. She is currently collaborating with a visual artist, with a joint collection of poetry and prints, *Up There Where the Air Is Rarefied*, forthcoming from Cinnamon Press in 2011. She is also one of the resident poets on BBC Radio 4's *Saturday Live*. Her website is at www.susanrichardsonwriter.co.uk.

Katharine Macrae

Katharine Macrae was born in Liverpool and educated at the University of Hull. She trained as a film editor with the BBC before becoming a script editor for BBC Northern Ireland. She worked with Eddie Izzard as the stylist on his *Definite Article* tour before becoming Head of Drama Development at Tiger Aspect Productions. Following the birth of her daughter she worked for nine years with the Liverpool playwright Alan Bleasdale as his researcher and editor. She has written a number of screenplays, currently in development. Katharine's first prose piece, *Another Place*, won a Field Report prize. 'Humber' is taken from her travelogue/memoir (work in progress). Katharine divides her time between Barcelona and the Llyn Peninsula in North Wales.

Ken Wilkie

Ken Wilkie is a Scottish writer based in The Netherlands. His drive to explore has taken him on travel assignments through many lands. Formerly a journalist working for *The Glasgow Herald*, *The Guardian* and *The Sunday Times*, he edited the KLM inflight magazine Holland Herald until 2004, when he was named Travel Journalist of the Year at the USA Travel Media Awards in London. His book *The Van Gogh File* has been translated into many languages.

Margaret Elphinstone

Margaret Elphinstone's latest novel, *The Gathering Night*, was published by Canongate in May 2009. She is the author of seven previous novels, including *The Sea Road, Hy Brasil, Voyageurs* and *Light*, as well as poetry, short stories, literary criticism and two books on organic gardening. She has spent her working life in various parts of Scotland including Shetland, Galloway, Edinburgh, Glasgow and Moray, and is Emeritus Professor in the Department of English Studies, University of Strathclyde. She has two daughters and three grandchildren and lives in Galloway with her partner.

Andrew Greig

Andrew Greig is the author of six collections of poetry, the latest of which is *This Life, This Life: New and Selected Poems*, published by Bloodaxe Books. His six novels are *That Summer, Electric Brae, The Return of John McNab, When They Lay Bare, In Another Light* and *Romanno Bridge*. After writing *Summit Fever* and *Kingdoms of Experience* about his Himalayan expeditions in the eighties, his latest work of nonfiction is *Preferred Lies,* a novel take on Golf and Life. 'Dub' will appear in *At the Loch of the Green Corrie* (Quercus, 2010) a book-length memoir and meditation on Norman MacCaig, Assynt, poetry and the natural and unnatural world. Andrew Greig lives in Edinburgh and Orkney.

Copyright Information

Two Ravens Press is the most northerly literary publisher in the UK, operating from a six-acre working croft on a sea-loch in the north-west Highlands of Scotland. Two Ravens Press is run by two writers with a passion for language and for books that are non-formulaic and that take risks. We publish cutting-edge and innovative contemporary fiction, non-fiction and poetry.

Visit our website for comprehensive information on all of our books and authors – and for much more:

- browse all Two Ravens Press books by category or by author, and purchase them online, post & packing-free (in the UK, and for a small fee overseas)

- there is a separate page for each book, including summaries, extracts and reviews, and author interviews, biographies and photographs

- read our regular blog about life as a small literary publisher in the middle of nowhere – or the centre of the universe, depending on your perspective – with a few anecdotes about life down on the croft thrown in. Includes regular and irregular columns by guest writers – Two Ravens Press authors and others

- sign up for our monthly e-newsletter, filled with information on our new releases and our authors, with special discounts, prizes and other offers.

www.tworavenspress.com